An account of the p

of Wallachia and Moldavia

with various political observations relating to them

William Wilkinson

Alpha Editions

This edition published in 2024

ISBN : 9789362998545

Design and Setting By
Alpha Editions
www.alphaedis.com
Email - info@alphaedis.com

As per information held with us this book is in Public Domain.
This book is a reproduction of an important historical work. Alpha Editions uses the best technology to reproduce historical work in the same manner it was first published to preserve its original nature. Any marks or number seen are left intentionally to preserve its true form.

PREFACE.

Amongst the nations of Europe most given to letters, none have so largely contributed to the general list of publications, relating to the condition and progress of the different countries of the world, as the English; and no travellers possess to the same degree as they do the love of describing them, however numerous the accounts that have preceded the period of their own experimental observations. Their journals, nevertheless, hardly ever fail to create interest, and the least share of novelty in form or matter induces the less travelling class of their countrymen to read them with pleasure.

Turkey and Egypt in particular have long been favourite themes; and indeed the Ottoman empire in every point of view, whether topographical, historical, administrative, religious, moral, political, military, or commercial, offers an inexhaustible subject for investigation, and an endless excitement to curiosity. No regular and minute description has, however, yet been undertaken of two of its most important and curious provinces, those which divide the principal part of the ancient kingdom of Dacia, under the modern denomination of Wallachia and Moldavia, although in the renewed existence of Greek governments exercising most of the prerogatives of independency, in the struggles of two nations between a strong remnant of Dacian barbarism and the influence of modern civilisation, and in a country comprehending within its own boundaries all the productive resources which fall but separately to the share of other countries, sufficient matter may be found to render them a subject by no means unworthy of notice.

These considerations have encouraged me to write the following pages with the view of laying them before the public. An official residence of some years in the principalities of Wallachia and Moldavia, afforded me the most ample opportunities of observation on every thing they contain most interesting, and I have endeavoured to make an accurate and satisfactory description of them. With regard to their history, I have only dwelt upon the most remarkable events, and have merely given it that extent to which its degree of importance seems entitled. I was apprehensive that longer and more minute details might be found tedious and unnecessary.

I regret, however, that at the time I wrote this account, I was not sufficiently prepared to enter into further particulars with respect to the minerals with which those countries abound; I intend, if I return to them, to bestow as much attention as possible to that particular object, and to make it the subject of a future separate treatise.

I am aware that my present undertaking is deserving of an abler pen; but as the character of nations can only be properly understood after some length of residence among them, I trust that the circumstances which place it to my lot, will make the apology of my intrusion, and become a motive of indulgence to its deficiencies in literary merit.

As Wallachia was the country of my fixed residence, I naturally chose it for the principal scene of my observations; and indeed the history of the two principalities is throughout so intimately connected, the form of their respective governments, the language, manners, and customs of the inhabitants, have ever been so much alike, that a description of the one renders a distinct account of the other superfluous.

The political importance to which these two provinces have risen since the reign of the ambitious Catherine, has given them a place of no small consequence in the general balance of Europe. Most of the European cabinets keep an eye upon them from the same motives, though with different views; but politics alone have hitherto brought them into notice, and philosophically or philanthropically speaking, it must be confessed that a share of attention, directed by common justice and humanity, was equally due to their definitive fate.

I have taken an opportunity of introducing into my appendix, a very curious account of the military system of the Ottoman empire, translated from a Turkish manuscript by an English gentleman, who possesses a perfect knowledge of that language, and who has favoured me with it. I have added to it some explanatory notes, rendered necessary by the metaphorical, and in many parts, obscure style of the original writing, and which my friend has purposely translated in a literal sense, in order not to divest it of that originality of narration which constitutes a great share of its interest.

The work was written in 1804, by order of the then reigning Sultan, Selim III., with the view of explaining the important advantages of the new military institution, called Nizam-y-Gedid, by which the Ottoman armies were trained into a regular form of discipline.

This institution, however necessary, and although strongly supported by all the higher classes, was so violently opposed by the clamorous janissaries, that at length it became impossible to continue it, and since the year 1805, the former regulations, or rather irregularities, have again been prevalent in the Ottoman armies. The same disorders which the Turkish author so faithfully describes as having existed before the introduction of the Nizam-y-Gedid, have necessarily followed its abolishment, and Turkey will no longer trust to her own means for salvation in future war. Her last one

with Russia has made her feel but too sensibly how far the present form of discipline of her armies may prove fatal to her existence, if ever she is abandoned to herself for defence.

CHAPTER I.
GEOGRAPHICAL POSITION AND EXTENT OF WALLACHIA AND MOLDAVIA—HISTORICAL REMARKS FROM THE DECLINE OF THE DACIANS TO THE LAST CENTURY.

The principalities of Wallachia and Moldavia, situated between 43° 40' and 48° 50' north latitude, 23° and 29° 30' east longitude, occupying a space of 350 miles in length, and 160 in breadth, are separated from the Austrian provinces of Temesvar, Transylvania, and Boukovina, by the Carpathian mountains; from Russia, by the river Pruth; and from Bulgaria (the ancient Mœsia), by the Danube.

It is sufficiently ascertained that these two provinces, joined to those of Transylvania and Temesvar, composed the kingdom of Dacia, finally conquered by the Romans.

The Dacians were originally a Scythian or Sarmatian tribe, resembling, in language and manners, the Thracians; the Greeks, indeed, considered them as a part of the Thracian nation.

They were a sober and vigorous people, capable of enduring any hardships and privations in war: they did not fear exposing themselves to the greatest dangers, because they looked upon death as the beginning of a much happier life; and this doctrine, according to Strabo, they held from a philosopher named Zamolxis, who was held in high repute by them.

The progress of the Roman arms, which, under the reign of Augustus, were carried to the banks of the Danube, brought them into contact with the Dacians, who were at that time governed by a warlike prince named Bærebestes, who boldly set the Roman conquerors at defiance. After his death, they were divided into four or five different principalities, and their strength was a good deal broken by the Romans; but their last king Decebalus, one of the ablest and most enterprising warriors of his time, re-united them into one body towards the 87th year of the Christian æra.

The first irruption of the Dacians into the territory of the empire, took place during the latter part of Augustus's reign; and, at times repulsed, at other times successful, they continued to annoy the Romans without any decisive advantage taking place on either side. At last the Emperor Domitian, determined to put a stop to their depredations, marched in person against them.

The particulars of the war which ensued are sufficiently detailed in the Roman history. The result of it having been such as to compel Domitian to sue for peace; he consented to pay to Decebalus an annual sum in the shape of a pension, but which, in fact, was nothing less than a tribute. It was regularly paid by the Romans until the year 102, when the Emperor Trajan declared his resolution to discontinue it; and the Dacians thereby considering themselves no longer bound to observe the treaty of peace, crossed the Danube, and laid waste the Roman territory. Upon these acts of hostility, Trajan put himself at the head of a numerous army, and marching against them, forced them to retire, passed the Danube in pursuit, engaged and defeated their successive forces, and finally compelled Decebalus to acknowledge himself his vassal. Trajan then returned to Rome, where he received the honour of a triumph, and the title of *Dacicus*.

But not long after, Decebalus, eager to shake off the Roman yoke, invaded and plundered the territory of his neighbours the Iazygæ, who were also tributary to the empire, on their refusal to join him against the Romans. Trajan again took the field at the head of a vast army, determined to chastise and subdue the Dacians. He reached the banks of the Danube in Autumn, and he thought it prudent to wait there the return of the fine season, that he might carry on military operations with more facility and success. It was during this interval, that he caused his famous bridge to be built over the Danube, under the direction of the architect Apollodorus of Damascus; and its present remains are sufficiently visible to verify the ancient accounts of this stupendous work. When the water is very low, some of the piles stand two or three feet above it, and render that part of the river difficult of navigation; they are looked upon as rocks by the natives of each side.

At the return of the Spring, when the bridge was completed, the Roman army marched over it, and commenced hostilities. The war was long and difficult, but it terminated in the complete subjugation of the Dacians, and in the death of their king, Decebalus, who, finding it impossible to avoid being made prisoner, killed himself that he might not fall alive into the conquerors' hands.

Dacia was thus converted into a Roman province, and Trajan shortly after sent colonies to increase its population. New cities were built, and pavements were constructed on the high roads, for the greater facility of communication.[1] It was governed by a Roman pro-prætor until the year 274.

Under the reign of Gallienus, when the empire was already declining, various parts of Dacia were seized by the Goths, and other barbarous nations.

A few Roman legions yet remained in the country, under the reign of the Emperor Aurelian, who, returning from Gaul, came down to Illyria, and finding a great part of Dacia in the hands of the barbarians, foresaw the impossibility of maintaining any possessions in the midst of them, and he withdrew a good number of the Roman inhabitants to the other side of the Danube, and settled them in Mæsia.

During the space of a hundred years from that period, those of the natives who had remained behind, and their descendants, were incessantly exposed to the rapacities of a variety of barbarous tribes, who came into the country for plunder.

Towards the year 361, the Goths, more powerful than the rest, seemed to have been left in exclusive possession of the province, and were inclined to make a permanent stay in it. They embraced the Christian religion, and established it in Dacia; since when, to the present moment, it has never ceased to be predominant amongst its inhabitants.

In 376, the Hunns, having over-run the countries possessed by the Goths, forced Athanaric, King of the Vizigoths, to retire with all his forces to that part of Dacia, situated between the rivers Dniester and Danube, now called Moldavia. He raised a wall between the latter river and the Pruth, by which he thought himself sufficiently protected against the attacks of his enemies. The Hunns, however, were not stopped by it; and their approach spread such consternation among the Goths of the interior, that those who had the means of escaping, to the number of some hundred thousand, fled for refuge into the Roman territory, and were permitted by the Emperor Valens, to settle in Thrace, upon condition that they should live peaceably there, and serve, when required, in the Roman armies.

The Hunns having penetrated into Dacia, were left masters of it until the year 453, when Ardaric, King of the Gepidæ, a people previously conquered by Attila and the Hunns, revolted against them, in consequence of Attila's death. His son and successor, Ellach, marched against them, but being defeated and slain, the Hunns were driven back into Scythia, and the Gepidæ remained masters of all Dacia. They entered into a sort of alliance with the Romans, who agreed to pay them a pension. In 550, their first quarrels with their neighbours, the Lombards, took place; and being sometimes assisted by the Emperor Justinian, they carried on frequent hostilities against them, for the space of eight years, at the end of which both nations resolved to decide the fate of the war by one great battle. The Lombards, under their King Alboin, had previously formed an alliance with the Avars, a people of Scythian extraction; and, assisted by them, they marched to action. Both sides fought with equal valor; but at last victory declared in favour of the Lombards, who, pursuing the Gepidæ, made a great slaughter among them. The Gepidæ, either destroyed, dispersed, or subdued, never after had a king of their own, and ceased to be a nation.

Alboin's achievements in Dacia attracted the notice of Narses, sent by Justinian to conquer Italy: he made offers to him, and finally engaged him to join the expedition with all his forces. The Lombards thus abandoned their possessions in Dacia and Pannonia to their friends and neighbours the Avars.

These, also known by the name of White-Hunns, remained in them until their own destruction by the Franks and Bulgarians. In the 7th century, being joined by other barbarous tribes, they pushed their incursions as far as the gates of Constantinople, where they were so completely defeated by the Emperor Heraclius, that they could not recover the blow: it was the original cause of their rapid decline.

Towards the close of the same century, a nation, known under the names of Slaves and Bulgarians, came from the interior of Russia to that part of Mæsia, which has since been called Bulgaria. Soon after a great number of Slaves, headed by their chief Krumo, crossed the Danube, and settled in Dacia, where they have since been known under the name of *Wallachs*. Opinion varies with respect to the origin of this name. Some historians pretend that the Slaves distinguished by it the Romans of Mæsia; whilst others maintain that they meant by it a people who led a pastoral life, and had given it to the inhabitants of Mæsia, most of whom were shepherds; and that a great number of these, having joined the Slaves in Dacia, the name by degrees became a general one amongst its inhabitants. The modern Wallachians, however, exclude it altogether from their language, and call themselves "Rumunn" or Romans, giving to their country the name of Roman-land, "Tsara-Rumaneska."

Some former inhabitants of Dacia, joined by a number of Slaves and Bulgarians, separated from the new settlers, and went to the lower part of Dacia lying between the rivers Olt and Danube, where they fixed their habitations. They formed themselves into a nation, and chose for their chief one *Bessarabba*, to whom they gave the Slavonic title of *Bann* or regent. The country within his jurisdiction was called *Bannat*; and it retains to this day the name of Bannat of Crayova, the latter being that of its present capital. Several other petty independent states arose at the same time in various parts of Dacia; but they were frequently annexed to the same sceptre, at other periods dismembered, according to the warlike ardour or indolence and incapacity of their various chiefs. Their general system, however, consisted in making war against the Romans of the lower empire, in which they were seconded by the Slaves and Bulgarians of Mæsia, whom they looked upon as their natural allies. This state of things continued to the close of the 9th century, at which period the Slaves having fallen into decline, various hordes, originally Scythians, successively undertook the conquest of Dacia, driving each other out of it, according to the momentary superiority of the one over the other. The most remarkable of these were the Hazars, the Patzinaces, the Moangoures, the Ouzes, the Koumans, and other Tartars.

The natives were treated as slaves by all these hordes of barbarian intruders, and great numbers of them were continually retiring to the other side of the Carpathians; where they settled under their own chiefs, sometimes independent, at others tributary to the kings of Hungary. The most conspicuous and thriving of these colonies were those of Fagarash and Maramosh.

The devastations continued in the plains finally drove out all the natives, and in the 11th century the Tartars retired, leaving the country a complete desert. It remained in this state until the year 1241, when the inhabitants of Fagarash, conducted by their chief Raddo Negro (Rodolphus the Black), crossed the mountains, and took possession of that tract of country, which is now called Upper Wallachia. Nearly at the same time, the inhabitants of Maramosh under their chief Bogdan, came and settled in that part which is by some called Moldavia, from the name of the river Moldau, which crosses it to fall into the Danube, and by the natives and Turks, Bogdania. Raddo Negro and his followers halted at the foot of the mountains, where they laid the foundation of a city, to which they gave the name of Kimpolung. At present it is reduced to an indifferent village; but its original extent is marked by old walls in ruin; and some inscriptions in its cathedral church attest it to have been Raddo's capital. His successors transferred their residence to Tirgovist, more pleasantly situated in the plains.

Some Wallachian, Transylvanian, and Hungarian authors differ in opinion with respect to the exact period of Raddo's and Bogdan's establishment in Wallachia and in Moldavia, and fix it at a different year of the early part of the 13th century; but as they give no satisfactory explanation on the subject, I am disposed to differ from them all, in placing that event in the year 1241, on the strength of the following considerations:—1st. It does not appear probable that the kings of Hungary, who, at the commencement of the 13th century were very powerful, and who looked upon Fagarash and Maramosh as dependencies of their crown, would have suffered their inhabitants to desert them, in order to settle in foreign countries: 2dly, It would seem strange that Raddo, Bogdan, and their followers should have quitted their homes in a prosperous country, and come to inhabit a desert, without some extraordinary event had necessitated so remarkable an emigration: and 3dly, the best Hungarian historians place in the year 1240 the invasion of Battou-Han in the northern countries; and add, that having crossed Russia and Poland at the head of 500,000 men, he entered Hungary in the year 1241, where he staid three years, during which he put every thing to fire and sword, and finally retired because nothing more was left to satisfy his thirst of blood.[2] It appears, then, extremely probable that the ravages of Battou-Han, and the terror he spread in the adjacent provinces, were the only causes of this emigration, which no historian has yet otherwise accounted for.

Bogdan and Raddo assumed the Slavonic title of Voïvode, equivalent to that of commanding prince. When tranquillity was restored in Hungary, they acknowledged the supremacy of the Hungarian king; but it does not appear that the formalities of the recognition had been such as to bind their successors; for, at the early part of the principalities, some Voïvodes disputed it with success; and from the commencement of the 14th century, their independency was acknowledged by Hungary.

The Bannat of Crayova had been little molested during the great incursions of the barbarians: in the 9th century it had become tributary to the kings of Hungary, who afterwards held it as a sort of refuge for the knights going to, and coming from, the Holy Land; but soon after Raddo's arrival, the Bann submitted to him the supreme sovereignty of the Bannat, and it has since then been annexed to the principality of Wallachia.

During the latter part of his life, Raddo raised another city, distant about thirty miles south-west of Kimpolung, on the borders of the river Argis: he gave it the name of Courté d'Argis, and resided in it occasionally. He also built a church here, which, two hundred years after, one of the Voïvodes beautified in a very conspicuous manner. The whole of the exterior work is entirely of carved marble, something in the style of the steeple of St. Stephen's church at Vienna, but far more elegant. The whole produces a very striking effect; and, as it has perfectly preserved its original beauty, it is certainly a monument that the Wallachians may boast of in any part of Europe.

The Voïvodate was not made hereditary; and although it devolved sometimes from father to son, the successor was obliged to go through the formality of being elected by the chiefs of the nation.

Several successors of Raddo strengthened the government, the population increased, and a great number of small towns and villages were built in the country. Frequent hostilities against the Hungarians, arising from the claims of sovereignty of the latter, accustomed the Wallachians to war; and in 1391 the Voïvoide Mirtza collected a numerous force, and attacked the neighbouring possessions of the Turks with the view of rescuing them from their hands. The Sultan Bajazet being at that moment employed in Asia in a troublesome war with the Prince of Castomona, had left his conquests near the Danube without the means of defence. But when the news of their invasion reached him, he suspended his operations in Asia, and returned to Adrianople, from whence he sent a numerous army to Wallachia. The Voïvode marched to meet the Turks; and, after a bloody battle, he was defeated, and compelled to become tributary to the Sultan. The annual amount of the tribute was fixed at three thousand piasters.[3]

Wallachia continued to pay it until the year 1444; when Ladislas King of Hungary, preparing to make war against the Turks, engaged the Voïvode Dracula to form an alliance with him. The Hungarian troops marched through the principality and were joined by four thousand Wallachians under the command of Dracula's son.[4]

The Hungarians being defeated at the celebrated battle of Varna, Hunniades their general, and regent of the kingdom during Ladislas's minority, returned in haste to make new preparations for carrying on the war. But the Voïvode, fearful of the Sultan's vengeance, arrested and kept him prisoner during a year, pretending thereby to show to the Turks that he treated him as an enemy. The moment Hunniades reached Hungary, he assembled an army and placed himself at the head of it, returned to Wallachia, attacked and defeated the Voïvode, and caused him to be beheaded in his presence; after which he raised to the Voïvodate one of the primates of the country, of the name of *Dan*.

The Wallachians under this Voïvode joined again the Hungarians in 1448, and made war on Turkey; but being totally defeated at the battle of Cossova, in Bulgaria, and finding it no longer possible to make any stand against the Turks, they submitted again to the annual tribute, which they paid until the year 1460, when the Sultan Mahomet II. being occupied in completing the conquest of the islands in the Archipelago, afforded them a new opportunity of shaking off the yoke. Their Voïvode, also named Dracula[5], did not remain satisfied with mere prudent measures of defence: with an army he crossed the Danube and attacked the few Turkish troops that were stationed in his neighbourhood; but this attempt, like those of his predecessors, was only attended with momentary success. Mahomet having turned his arms against him, drove him back to Wallachia, whither he pursued and defeated him. The Voïvode escaped into Hungary, and the Sultan caused his brother Bladus to be named in his place. He made a treaty with Bladus, by which he bound the Wallachians to perpetual tribute; and laid the foundations of that slavery, from which no efforts have yet had the power of extricating them with any lasting efficacy. The following is the substance of the treaty:—

1. "The Sultan consents and engages for himself and his successors, to give protection to Wallachia, and to defend it against all enemies, assuming nothing more than a supremacy over the sovereignty of that principality, the Voïvodes of which shall be bound to pay to the Sublime Porte an annual tribute of ten thousand piasters."

2. "The Sublime Porte shall never interfere in the local administration of the said principality, nor shall any Turk be ever permitted to come into Wallachia without an ostensible reason."

3. "Every year an officer of the Porte shall come to Wallachia to receive the tribute, and on his return shall be accompanied by an officer of the Voïvode as far as Giurgevo on the Danube, where the money shall be counted over again, a second receipt given for it, and when it has been carried in safety to

the other side of that river, Wallachia shall no longer be responsible for any accident that may befall it."[6]

4. "The Voïvodes shall continue to be elected by the archbishop, metropolitan, bishops, and boyars[7], and the election shall be acknowledged by the Porte."

5. "The Wallachian nation shall continue to enjoy the free exercise of their own laws; and the Voïvodes shall have the right of life and death over their own subjects, as well as that of making war and peace, without having to account for any such proceedings to the Sublime Porte."

6. "All Christians who, having once embraced the Mahometan faith, should come into Wallachia and resume the Christian religion, shall not be claimed by any Ottoman authorities."

7. "Wallachian subjects who may have occasion to go into any part of the Ottoman dominions, shall not be there called upon for the haratsh or capitation tax paid by other *Rayahs*."[8]

8. "If any Turk have a lawsuit in Wallachia with a subject of the country, his cause shall be heard and decided by the Wallachian divan, conformably to the local laws."

9. "All Turkish merchants coming to buy and sell goods in the principality, shall, on their arrival, have to give notice to the local authorities of the time necessary for their stay, and shall depart when that time is expired."

10. "No Turk is authorised to take away one or more servants of either sex, natives of Wallachia; and no Turkish mosque shall ever exist on any part of the Wallachian territory."

11. "The Sublime Porte promises never to grant a Ferman[9] at the request of a Wallachian subject for his affairs in Wallachia, of whatever nature they may be; and never to assume the right of calling to Constantinople, or to any other part of the Turkish dominions, a Wallachian subject on any pretence whatever."

This treaty in many respects advantageous to Wallachia, still forms the basis of its constitution. The first, third, fourth, and latter part of the fifth articles only, have since undergone alterations, which have proved in no small degree detrimental to the liberties of that country. The remainder have been, and are to this day, punctually observed.

The qualification of a mere tributary prince did not, however, appear to the Sultan Mahomet as implying sufficient submission; and, in order to place the person of the Voïvode under a more immediate dependence, he gave him the rank and title of a Turkish Pashah; a dignity, which has ever since been inseparable from that of Voïvode or Hospodar.

The principality remained in a peaceable state several years after its war with Mahomet, and the weakness and incapacity of several of its princes afforded to the Ottoman court the means of ruling over it with increasing power. In 1544 portions of territory bordering on the Danube were ceded to the Turks; the fortresses of Ibraïl, Giurgevo, and Tourno, which have much figured in all the subsequent European wars of Turkey, were raised upon them, and were garrisoned by Turkish soldiers. Having gained so strong a footing in the country, the conduct of the Turks became more and more overbearing: its rights and privileges were no longer respected; and the Porte countenanced, or connived at, every sort of depredation committed by the soldiers of the garrisons beyond the boundaries of the fortresses; and soon treated the principality and its inhabitants as on the same footing with all its other Christian conquests.

This state of things continued to the year 1593, when an individual of the name of Michael was elected to the Voïvodate. He no sooner held the reins of government than he determined to deliver his country from the Turkish yoke, and restore it to independency. Circumstances soon afforded him an opportunity of putting this plan into execution. The Prince Sigismund of Transylvania, also tributary to the Turks, revolted against them towards this period, at the instigations of the Pope and of the Emperor Rodolphus. With him and with the Voïvode Aaron of Moldavia, Michael formed a league against the enemies of Christianity. But in order to give a greater appearance of justice to their proceedings, the allies sent a long list of grievances to the Porte, demanded redress, and insisted that some satisfactory guarantee were given of a change of system for the future. These representations not only remained unanswered, but, shortly after they were made, a troop of three thousand Janissaries came into Wallachia, and went about the country, levying contributions on the villagers, and committing all sorts of outrages. A Wallachian force was at last sent against them, and they were all put to the sword; after which, Michael, at the head of an army composed of his own troops and those of his allies, marched against Giurgevo, and compelled its garrison to retire to the other side of the Danube.

The threatening attitude of Michael and his allies induced the Sultan Amurat to desist from further provocation, and to wait for a more favourable moment of imposing again his yoke on the principalities; but he died suddenly in 1595, and his successor, Mahomet III., no sooner ascended the throne than he resolved to carry that plan into execution by the means of an overpowering army. Forty thousand Turks and twenty thousand Tartars, under the orders of the Grand Vezier, invaded the Wallachian and Moldavian provinces nearly at the same time, and a long war ensued. The invaders suffered a series of defeats: for five years they renewed the campaign with no better success; and the Sultan was finally compelled to relinquish his claims.

In 1600, after the abdication of Sigismund of Transylvania, that principality became tributary to the Emperor Rodolphus; and as the Voïvode Michael, whom the emperor had engaged into his interests, had assisted him in defeating the schemes of Cardinal Battori, pretender to the Transylvanian sovereignty, Rodolphus, to reward him, left him the government of Transylvania. The Voïvode fixed his residence in that province, and appointed a lieutenant in Wallachia. But in the following year the Transylvanians, not satisfied with his administration, revolted, and sent invitations to their former Prince, Sigismund, who was living as a private individual at Clausenburg, to come and resume the supreme authority. An Austrian army, under the command of General Baste, was hastily dispatched to stop the progress of the rebellion; and Michael, who had repaired to Wallachia, returned with some troops, and joined the imperial general. They marched together against the rebels, who had formed an army of equal strength, and an obstinate battle took place, which terminated in the entire defeat of the insurgents, and in the subjection of the whole province. When events had determined the fate of Transylvania, the two allied commanders quarrelled in a discussion concerning the ulterior measures of administration; and Baste, resolved by some means or other to get rid of Michael, whose pretensions appeared to him to have become of a dangerous tendency, caused him to be assassinated. The Wallachian troops were sent back to their country, and they carried away with them the head of the Voïvode Michael, which was buried in the monastery of *Dialloluy*, near the town of Tirgovist, where the monument that was placed over it at the time, with an inscription alluding to the principal events of his life, and to the circumstances of his death, engraved in Slavonian characters, still exists.

The death of Michael, which took place in 1602, spread great consternation and confusion in Wallachia. The Primates[10] lost time in deliberations on the measures that were to be pursued; and the Turkish Pashahs of the neighbourhood sent a strong body of troops, which, crossing the Danube at different places, occupied the greatest part of the principality, and put it out of the power of the Wallachians to make any effectual resistance. The sultan's orders for the election of a Voïvode of his own choice were soon obeyed, and the principality resumed its tributary character; the treaty of Mahomet II. was renewed, but the amount of the tribute was fixed at a much higher sum. From this period forward, Wallachia remained under the power of the Ottoman Sultans; and although its inhabitants, in the course of the 17th century, made frequent efforts to throw off the yoke, the success of such attempts always proved momentary, and consequently more injurious than beneficial to them in the sequel.

With regard to Moldavia, the first act of its submission to the Turks was not the effect of conquest, but a voluntary measure of precaution and security.[11] It was only in 1536 that this principality consented to become tributary to the Sultan, and the event is thus explained by all the Moldavian historians.

In 1529 the Voïvode Stephen, being on his death-bed, called to him his son Bogdan, who was likely to succeed him, and his principal nobles: he addressed them at length on the political situation of the country, representing the probability of its being soon attacked by the Turks, and the insufficiency of its means to make any effectual resistance against their power. He dwelt on the ferocious character of the reigning Sultan Suleÿman I., and recommended to them in the strongest manner, rather to seek his clemency by the voluntary offer of a tribute, than expose themselves to his vengeance in resisting his attempts to obtain it.

After Stephen's death, Bogdan neglected some years his father's advice, till at last he saw the necessity of following it; and he sent, in 1536, ambassadors to Constantinople to offer the tribute. The Sultan then entered into written engagements with him, by which the same privileges as those of Wallachia were granted to Moldavia; but in which the tribute was merely called a *Peshkicsh*, or present.

Moldavia was governed on the same plan as the sister province, and frequently shared the same fate in war; sometimes ravaged by the Turks, at other times successful in resisting them. Towards the close of the 16th century, after its successful co-operation with Wallachia, Sigismund of Transylvania seized it, deposed the Voïvode Aaron, his friend and ally, and appointed a man of his own choice, whom he bound to pay him tribute. But in 1597, a Polish army invaded the province, and rescued it from the hands of Sigismund. In 1602 the Poles restored it to the Turks, against whose power the Moldavians never after struggled with any permanent success. Their frequent and fruitless efforts to regain independency, exhausted their means and patriotic ardour; and by degrees they became accustomed to the Turkish yoke. The appointment of the Voïvodes was left to the pleasure of the Sultans, although the formality of the election continued to take place a long time after; but the tribute was no longer called a present, and its amount was increased at almost every new appointment.

As far, however, as the end of the 17th century, intervening political motives still induced the Porte to show some deference to the privileges of the two principalities; but at the early part of the 18th century, the Ottoman Court became less constrained in its policy, and in assuming the right of punishing by death the Wallachian princes, laid the foundations of that system by which both have been governed to the present moment. The event which proved so fatal to the respective constitutions of those states, will show at the same time how far their public spirit must have been subdued, and how rapid appears to have been its decline.

During the reign of Sultan Ahmet, the Porte had, in 1695, declared war against the Emperor; and the Voïvode Constantine Brancovano Bessarabba of Wallachia was directed to form an army, and to march into the Austrian states, in order to second the operations of the Grand Vizier who was to commence hostilities from the frontiers of Servia. The Voïvode partly obeyed; but, either from a secret hatred to the Turks, or from being bribed into the Emperor's cause, probably from both these motives, he abstained from taking any active part in the campaign, and by that circumstance alone, favoured the operations of the Austrians. At the conclusion of the peace of Carlowitz, the Emperor Leopold rewarded the Voïvode's services by conferring on him the title of Prince of the Roman Empire, together with the gift of some landed estates in Transylvania. These circumstances could not remain hidden from the knowledge of the Ottoman court, who, however, found it necessary to use dissimulation; and some years elapsed without any notice being taken of them.

In 1710, Bessarabba was drawn into a secret correspondence with the Czar Peter the great, the object of which was to obtain his co-operation in that sovereign's projected war against the Turks. The Voïvode promised a contingent of thirty thousand men, and an ample supply of provisions and other necessaries for the Russian army.

The purport of this correspondence became known to the Porte, and the death of Bessarabba was immediately determined upon; but at the same time it was deemed adviseable to use stratagem instead of open force, and it was resolved that he should be drawn into a snare by the Prince of Moldavia. Nicholas Marrocordato then governed that province, but he was thought unfit for the execution of the plan; the Porte therefore recalled him, and appointed to the principality Demetrius Cantimir, whose fidelity had been frequently tried both in peace and war. Cantimir set out from Constantinople for Moldavia, having instructions and positive orders to seize Bessarabba under the colour of friendship, alliance, or any pretence which he might think proper, and send him alive or dead to Constantinople.[12]

But Cantimir, who, it seems, had neither the ambition nor the desire of being made Voïvode of Moldavia, having twice before procured that principality to his younger brother Antiochus, accepted it with the express condition that he should not be called upon to pay any tribute, or to make any of the presents customary at the new nominations. But when he reached Moldavia the Grand Vezier wrote to him by the Sultan's order, not only to send immediately the usual tribute and presents, but also to prepare provisions for a numerous Turkish army, to throw a bridge over the Danube for their passage, and to join the Turks in person with Moldavian troops, besides other intolerable burthens.[13] Cantimir says, that perceiving now how little faith was to be expected from the infidels, and esteeming it far better to suffer for the Christian cause, he resolved to detach himself from the Turkish interest, and sent a faithful messenger to the Czar, with an offer of his services and principality.

With these favourable prospects in Wallachia and in Moldavia, the Czar advanced towards the Ottoman frontiers. In 1711, he arrived with all his forces at Yassi, where he remained some days in expectation of the contingent and provisions promised by the Voïvode of Wallachia. But it seems that Bessarabba, as the rupture between the Sultan and the Czar drew near, alarmed at the great preparations of the Turks, and the approach of their army, composed of two hundred and twenty thousand men, thought it prudent to take no part in the war, and the subsequent disasters of the Russians are in a great measure attributed to the failure of his former promises to the Czar, who had placed too great a reliance in them. The events of this war are too well known to need any further explanation here. When peace was restored, and the Voïvodate of Moldavia had remained vacant by Cantimir's defection, Nicholas Marrocordato was again appointed to it. Bessarabba remained unmolested, but not without the fear of early vengeance. Eager to regain the favour of the Ottoman government, and to obtain the assurance of oblivion on the past, he sent large supplies of money, and considerable presents to the Turkish ministers, and to the public treasures; he repeated them so often, as to convince the court that he possessed immense wealth, and the Grand Vezier, Ally-Pashah, who was his personal enemy, obtained from the Sultan a formal order for his recall, and for the seizure of his treasures. The Vezier then formed the plan of enforcing this order, and it was carried into execution in the following manner:—

In 1714, at the beginning of April, being the week of the Passion, when the attention of the Wallachians and their occupations were entirely devoted to the long ceremonies of the Greek church, a Capigee-Bashi[14], of the Sultan, arrived at Bukorest with a suite of a hundred men; he sent word to the Voïvode that he was on his way to Hotim upon very pressing business of the state, and that he should only have time to pay him a visit on the next morning, after which he intended to take his departure. Accordingly, he went the next day to the palace, and, on entering the closet of the Voïvode, who stood up to receive him, he placed a black handkerchief on his shoulder, conformably to the then usual method of announcing depositions to persons high in office in Turkey. The Voïvode was confounded by the unexpected compliment, but the moment he recovered from his first emotions, he burst into a long strain of invectives against the Sultan and the Turks, for treating him with so much ingratitude after the many services he had rendered to the

Porte. The Capigee, however, placed a guard about his person, and proceeded to the divan chamber, where he read a *Ferman*, which contained the decree of Bessarabba's deposition, declared him a traitor, and ordered him to Constantinople with all his family. After the *Ferman* had been published, the Capigee secured the public treasure, and all the Voïvode's private property. The frightened inhabitants of Bukorest remained tranquil spectators of all these acts of violence, and made no effort to release the Voïvode from his imprisonment. With a nation more awakened to its own dignity, and to the value of independence, an event of this nature would not, perhaps, have taken place without the support of an army, and the shedding of blood; and, indeed, the circumstances of this very occurrence would hardly appear credible, if they were not almost fresh in the memory of the present generation.

Two days after Bessarabba's deposition, one Stephen Cantacuzene, of Greek origin, and calling himself a descendant of the imperial family of that name[15], was, by the Sultan's order, raised to the Voïvodate.

On the 14th April, the Capigee-Bashi left Bukorest with Bessarabba, his wife, four sons, three daughters, and grandson, and escorted by the Turkish guard. They soon reached Constantinople, and the Voïvode, with all his family, was immediately confined in the state prison of the Seven Towers. His treasures not being found so considerable as had been expected, his sons were put to the torture for three successive days, that they might confess where their father had hidden the rest; or that the latter, being a witness to his children's torments, might come forward and make that confession himself. But as these cruelties did not produce the intended effect, the Sultan, exasperated at the apparent obstinacy of the sufferers, ordered them to be executed in his presence. The prisoners were conducted to a square, under the windows of the seraglio, and a long list of accusations was read to them; it alluded particularly to the treachery of Bessarabba in the Austrian war, and to the indignant expressions he had made use of against the person of the Sultan, when his recall had been signified to him. The four sons were first beheaded, one after the other, and the execution of the father closed this scene of butchery. When the Sultan withdrew, the five heads were put upon pikes, and carried about the streets of Constantinople. The bodies were thrown into the sea, but they were picked up by some Christian boatmen, and conveyed to a Greek monastery in the little island of Halcky, in the Propontis, where they received burial.

As to the unfortunate princess and the remainder of her family, they were shortly after exiled to Cuttaya, in Asia Minor, but three years after they were permitted to return to Wallachia.[16]

The Voïvode Cantacuzene only remained in office two years, and he was the last Wallachian prince, whose nomination was effected through the formality of election. This important prerogative of the inhabitants had been abolished some years before in Moldavia. The Porte found it unnecessary to suffer it any longer in Wallachia, and indeed it had, since more than a century, become merely nominal.

Nicholas Marrocordato was transferred from the government of Moldavia to that of Wallachia, and proclaimed by a Turkish Capigee-Bashi in 1716. At this time the Porte was preparing to carry on a defensive war against Austria; and had the primates of Wallachia felt the courage to protest against so manifest a violation of their privileges, they would, most probably, have succeeded in securing a better observance of them.

Since the commencement of the decline of the Turkish power, the Ottoman court has made it an invariable policy to infringe little by little on the privileges allowed to foreign nations by treaty; and to conduct, by systematic stratagem, an administration which has been constantly falling in vigour and energy. If any infraction is left unnoticed by the party it concerns, and the article of a treaty, in its modified state, is once applied with success to any case to which it may relate, it becomes a precedent which the Porte will obstinately refer to at any other time that the strict interpretation of the article is insisted upon.

Thus, without assigning any satisfactory reason, and without repealing, in a plausible manner, the Wallachian law of election, the Sultan took to himself the exclusive right of appointing to the two Voïvodates. The measure was not opposed, and its repetition became habitual; and if, at the present moment, the inhabitants of the two Principalities were to recall their right to memory, and claim the enforcement of it, the Porte would consider and treat the proceeding as open rebellion on their part.

No prince of Wallachian or Moldavian birth or origin, was ever appointed after the recall of Bessarabba, and the Porte would have been willing to govern the principalities through the means of Turkish Pashahs; but the intrigues of the state-interpreter, Alexander Marrocordato, who was then endeavouring to secure either of the Voïvodates to his son Nicholas, induced at the time the Ottoman government to introduce another system, which subsequent motives have contributed to support to the present day. The Porte selected the new princes from the Greeks of Constantinople, whose long habit of obedience and servile degradation, appeared to render them suitable tools for the new policy adopted, relative to the government of the principalities. From that moment the princes have been appointed by *Beratt*, an imperial diploma, in which the Sultan, in proclaiming the nominations, commands the Wallachian and Moldavian nations to acknowledge and obey the bearers of it, as sole depositories of the sovereign authority.[17]

They were instructed to pursue the plan, of administration of the Voïvodes, and thus they were suffered to hold a court, to confer dignities and titles of nobility, and to keep up a show of sovereign splendour, circumstances which were most flattering to the vanity of the Greeks, and proved useful to the interested views of the Porte. But they were most strictly forbidden to maintain troops, or to collect any, under any pretence whatever. This precaution was indispensable, as it prevented the princes from acquiring military power, and the natives from aspiring to independency.

In the course of the last century, a variety of Greek princes succeeded to each other in the government of the principalities. One alone, Constantine Marrocordato, appointed in 1735 to Wallachia, devoted himself with zeal to the welfare of the country. Some wise institutions, to which we shall have occasion to advert in the sequel, attest the liberality of his views, and a generosity of character which is not to be traced in any of his successors. But he was twice recalled, because he refused to comply with demands of the Ottoman government, which appeared to him incompatible with duties he owed to the Wallachians. The other princes, less scrupulous, and more careful of their own interests, marked their administration by the most violent acts of extortion, and an invariable system of spoliation. Few of them died of natural death, and the Turkish scymetar was, perhaps, frequently employed with justice among them. In a political point of view, the short reigns of most of these princes offer nothing of sufficient importance or interest to deserve a place in history.

CHAPTER II.
INAUGURATION OF THE HOSPODARS—PRESENT FORM OF GOVERNMENT—LOCAL LAWS—TRIBUNALS OF JUSTICE—MEMBERS OF THE DIVAN AND OTHER PUBLIC FUNCTIONARIES—DISTRICTS—CAÏMACAM OF CRAYOVA—ISPRAVNIKS.

The princes of Wallachia and Moldavia, since the choice of them falls on the Greeks, receive their investiture at the Porte, with the pomp and ceremonies usually observed on creating *Pashahs* and *Veziers*. The *Kukka*, or military crest, is put on their heads by the *Muzhur Aga*, and the robe of honour is put on them by the Vezier himself. They are honoured with the standards and military music, and make their oaths of allegiance in the presence of the Sultan, to whom they are introduced with the ceremonies usual at a public audience. From the seraglio, they go in solemn and ostentatious procession to the patriarchal church, where prayers and ceremonies are performed similar to those which were formerly observed at the inauguration of the Greek Emperors. They are accompanied to their principalities by the Turkish officers appointed to install them. They make their public entry into the capital of their new sovereignty with a great display of magnificence, attended by the metropolitan and dignified ecclesiastics, the members of the divan, and the chief Boyars. They assume, from the ceremonies which are practised, the title of "God's Anointed."[18]

The general form of government in both principalities has undergone little alteration since the exclusion of the native Voïvodes. The prince is invested with absolute authority, and, till lately, was only controllable in his financial operations, by the divan, representing the senate; still, in levying extraordinary contributions, and in fixing the mode of raising them, the signatures of a majority of members are required as a mere formality; and, although the want of these would render such acts illegal, they would not thereby be put with less vigour into execution.

The executive administration is divided into various regular departments. The divan, composed of twelve members, is the supreme council, and is presided by the Prince, who appoints to it new members every year, with the exception of the metropolitan, whose ecclesiastical dignity entitles him to a permanent seat. It is convened at least twice a week, to receive, examine, and decide upon appeals in judiciary matters.

A Voïvode of the name of Mathew Bessarabba, who governed Wallachia from 1633 to 1644, instituted laws which he drew from Justinian's code, and modified by the customs of the country. His example was soon after followed in Moldavia. Several princes made alterations in the original codes, and the late princes, Caradja of Wallachia, and Callimacki of Moldavia, have made them undergo a new revision, and have published them under their own names.[19] It is in conformity to these laws that all suits are said to be judged, and the sentences framed; but the prince interprets them in his own way, and his will, in fact, is the only predominating law.

The princes' decisions are without appeal for the natives of the country; and, however irregular or unjust they may be, they cannot be revoked by their successors.

In any case of moment, where the opinion of the members of the divan happens to be unanimous against that of the prince, or contrary to his wishes, the decision of the question is postponed, and the members are privately desired to pronounce according to the views of the prince. As they are aware that non-compliance would be attended with dismissal and disgrace, it is common enough, on similar occasions, that at the next sessions they all declare an opinion directly opposite to the one they had last given.

At Bukorest, and at Yassi, where the princes reside, there are two particular tribunals appropriated to the revision of commercial and other differences existing between the natives and foreign subjects. They are called the Foreign Departments, and are each directed by a Boyar, who has the title of chancellor of foreign affairs, and two other judges. The business that comes before them is examined and discussed in the presence of an officer attached to the consulate, by which the foreign party concerned is protected. The decisions are, conformably to the general sense of the treaties existing between the Porte and foreign powers, made according to the local laws; but they are not valid without the prince's confirmation, which can be withheld, and a timely appeal made either to the Grand Vezier's tribunal at Constantinople, or to the prince's own judgement, should the nature of the department's decision bear the appearance of partiality or injustice against the foreign party. Cases of this nature are so common, that the consuls are frequently obliged to act the part of attorneys in defending the rights of the individuals who are entitled to their protection.

There are also separate departments for the police, the treasury, and criminal cases, as well as a variety of petty offices for the different business, most of which report directly to the prince, and receive his instructions.

The following is an exact list of the chief dignitaries, and the other officers of state, according to their respective ranks and precedence, beginning with the twelve members of the divan.

The Metropolitan, or archbishop.

The Banno, a title taken from the former Banns of Crayova.

Vornik de Tsara de Suss, or judge of the upper country.

Vornik de Tsara de Joss, or judge of the lower country.

Logothett, or chancellor and keeper of the great seal.

3d *Vornik*, Common judges at the divan.
4th *Vornik*,

Logothett de Obichëy; his particular business consists in assembling the divan.

Vornik de Couttee, or treasurer for the pensions of the widows of poor Boyars.

Vornik de Politia, or collector of the capitation tax within the city of Bukorest.

Clutshiar, or keeper of the code of laws.

Clutshiar d'Aria; although he has a seat, he is not allowed to vote. He is a kind of sergeant-at-arms.

According to old custom, an individual, who is not born or naturalised a Wallachian or Moldavian, cannot be admitted member of the divan.

The first Postelnik is principal minister and master of the ceremonies at court. His office is of the most confidential nature, and only given to Greeks, near relations, or intimate friends of the prince.

The Spathar; his office formerly corresponded to that of minister at war. At present he is director-general of the police throughout the principality. In Moldavia he is more properly called *Hetman*.

The Vestiar, or treasurer of the principality: he must be a native.

The Hetman; in Wallachia his business consists in carrying into execution the prince's sentences in matters of judicature. He takes 10 *per cent.* on the value of the objects to which they relate.

Camarash, or first chamberlain; the prince's private treasurer, and judge over the Jews. He levies a duty upon all merchandise sold by retail for his own profit.

Armash, or judge of criminal causes relating to the lower orders; he has the superintendency of the public prisons, and collects the tribute paid by the gypsies to government.

Agga, or chief of the police within the city of Bukorest.

Portar-Bashi; he directs the correspondence with the neighbouring Turkish Pashahs, and other governors. He also attends upon all the Turks of distinction who visit Bukorest.

All the preceding offices give the rank of Boyars of the First Class to the persons who are appointed to them, and as such they wear their beards; they are all removed every year; but as they retain the titles until promotion, those in activity are distinguished from them by the additional one of *"great,"*—*"maray,"*—such as *Logothett-maray*, the Great Chancellor, &c.

The Boyars of the Second Class are as follows:—

Caminar, or collector of duties upon wine, brandy, tobacco, and snuff, brought to Bukorest for sale.

Paharnik, or cup-bearer. At state dinners he stands behind the prince's chair, and offers him to drink.

Comisso, or master of the horse.

Stolnik, chief steward at court.

Sardar, chief or colonel of the guards.

Third Class:—

Medelnitsher; he receives the petitions addressed to the Hospodars, and reads all the papers at the divan.

Pittar, superintendent of the prince's equipages.

Sludgier; he was formerly commissary to the regiment of body-guards: it is now an empty title.

Shatrar, keeper of the prince's tents.

2d Logothett 2d Postelnik 2d Vestiar 3d Logothett 3d Postelnik 3d Vestiar	All these are public clerks attached to the offices from which they derive their titles.

The renewal of public officers every year naturally creates great confusion in the transaction of public business. The custom arises from the circumstance that the Boyars, whose number in Wallachia amounts to nearly thirty thousand, claim public employment, at least, for a time, as a right to which they are each entitled. The first families, in particular, consider it as their birthright; but as their chief object is gain, they scramble for places with the most indecorous avidity, and never regard their want of capacity for any branch of public service.

As every Boyar has some title or other, he is never addressed by his name in common intercourse, but by his title preceded by the ancient Greek one of "ἄρχον," such as "Archon-Banno, Archon-Shatrar," &c.

A certain ceremony is practised at court upon all promotions and nominations. It takes place once or twice every month, when the prince, seated on an elevated throne, verbally notifies to the candidate, who is introduced by the First Postelnik, the rank or office to which he raises him. A robe of honour is then placed on his shoulders, and he advances in the most respectful attitude, and kisses the prince's hand. He is then conveyed home in one of the state-carriages, or on one of the prince's horses (according to his new rank) and accompanied by a great number of Chiohadars, or livery-servants of the court, to whom he pays a considerable fee.

The Boyars of the First Class look upon their titles as corresponding to those of Count and Baron in Germany, and their rank to that of Major-general in Russia. It is true that the Empress Catherine, at the period of her first war with Turkey, issued an Ukase to that effect; but her successors have set it aside. Although most of the principal families indulge the idea that none in Europe can boast of more genuine nobility, there are very few who can trace their origin any farther than a century back.[20] The present descendants of Bessarabba and Cantacuzene are amongst this number. A family in Wallachia bear the name of Paleologos, and confidently assert being descended from the race of the last Constantine. It would not be very material to attempt to refute such pretensions; few could be imposed upon by them. They appear, however, the more absurd, as the persons who make them cannot in any manner explain upon what grounds they are assumed.

Wallachia is divided into seventeen districts, including the Bannat of Crayova composed of five. They are called *Rimnik, Buzéo, Sakoyéni, Prahova, Yallomitza, Ilfov, Dimbovitza, Vlaska, Telly-Orman, Mousstzello, Argis, Olt, Romanatz, Vultza, Doltz, Gorge, Méhédintz*. Each of them is governed by two *Ispravniks* or deputies, whose appointment is renewed every year by the prince. Their business chiefly consists in collecting the tribute and other contributions, which they send to the *Vestiary*, from which they are in a great measure dependent. The *Ispravniks* of the Bannat are under the immediate orders of a lieutenant of the prince, who resides at Crayova, under the title of *Caïmacam*. The Greek princes have substituted this appointment to that of the *Banns*, taking the title from that of the Turkish minister who fills the office of the Grand Vezier at Constantinople during the latter's absence.

The situation of *Caïmacam* at Crayova is very lucrative, and generally given to some of the Greeks who follow the princes into Wallachia with the hope of enriching themselves.

The Ispravnicates are also given to persons of that description, jointly with the sons of Boyars, who, at a very early age, commonly make their *début* in public career by those appointments. They receive a salary of five hundred piasters per month, besides which they have perquisites, which, in some of the richest districts, they extend as far as twenty thousand piasters a year.

CHAPTER III.
POPULATION.—TRIBUTE AND TAXES.—OTHER BRANCHES OF REVENUE.—METROPOLITAN DIGNITY.—MONASTERIES.

The exact number of population in the two principalities has never been properly ascertained; but the nearest calculation approaches to one million of souls in Wallachia, and five hundred thousand in Moldavia, since the last peace of Bukorest.

This population is, in each principality, divided into three distinct classes; the Boyars, or nobles, of the different orders; the tradesmen of all descriptions; and the peasants, with others, who are liable to the common taxes and contributions.

All the male peasants are, by their birth, subject to the capitation tax, from the age of sixteen; with the exception of some few who compose a privileged body called *Sokotelniki*, they are divided into associations called *Loods*, each of which is composed of a certain number of individuals, from five to ten, according to their respective means, and pays a fixed sum of six hundred piasters every year to the prince. According to the registers of the Wallachian Vestiary in 1818, the total of the *loods* in the seventeen districts, amounted to eighteen thousand, which, at the rate of six hundred piasters, gave an annual income of 10,800,000 piasters.[21] This amount of revenue is considered as becoming the property of the reigning prince, and not as due by the inhabitants to the Ottoman government, as some writers have represented.

The treaties made by Mahomet II. and Suleÿman I. in leaving to Wallachia and to Moldavia the power of choosing their own princes, bound these alone to pay an annual tribute; the amount of it was at different periods increased; but it is now fixed at two millions of piasters for Wallachia, and one million for Moldavia. The Porte has indeed broken its original engagements by assuming the exclusive right of giving to those countries Greek princes instead of their own; but in doing so, the Ottoman court did not degrade the character of sovereignty inherent in the native Voïvodes; and if the present princes did not bear that character, their decisions would not be, as they are, without appeal for the natives.

The policy of the Porte, and the precarious position of the Greek Hospodars, have, however, for a long time rendered the fixed amount of the tribute due to the Porte merely nominal; and it is perfectly understood that the latter, on receiving their appointments, engage to satisfy any calls of the Turkish government, of money and other necessaries.

Besides the *loods*, there are in Wallachia about one hundred thousand individuals, and a proportionable number in Moldavia, who do not belong to the class of peasants, but who pay taxes at an equal rate. These are the tradesmen, Ottoman Jews, and other Rayahs.

The privileged class called *Sokotelniki* is composed of fifteen thousand individuals taken from among the peasantry, and who were, till lately, perfectly exempted from every kind of contribution levied by government; but within a few years the greater number of them have been made liable to an annual capitation tax of twenty piasters each.

Their institution dates its origin from a remarkable reform made by Constantine Mavrocordato, in 1736, when he had the government of both principalities at the same time.

Until that period, most of the peasants were slaves of the Boyars: Mavrocordato abolished the system, and no attempt was ever made since to renew it. In order, however, to indemnify in some measure the Boyars for the loss of their slaves, he regulated that each should be allowed to exact from a limited number of his peasants an annual tribute, in any shape whatever; and that this class of peasants, to whom he gave the name of Sokotelniki, should be entirely exempted from the burthen of public imposts.

Every Boyar of the first rank is now entitled to eighty Sokotelniki, each of whom pays him the annual sum of eighty piasters; some few, instead of receiving money, employ their Sokotelniki in the cultivation of their lands, and thus derive a much greater advantage from them.

The privilege, however, is not hereditary either with the possessors, or the private tributary. Every rank had a fixed number; and by the inattention and neglect of many princes, as well as by the unceasing increase of titles of nobility, the Sokotelniki became so numerous, that in 1814 the government in Wallachia determined to allow no longer to private individuals a considerable amount of revenue which could be appropriated to its own use. A new law was therefore made, which formed into government-loods all Sokotelniki who were not attached to the first class of Boyars. The institution of this law was warmly supported by the members of the divan, who, with their equals, had no loss to apprehend; but it created great discontent in all the other classes affected by it, and particularly with the Boyars of Crayova, who being more given to agricultural occupations than the other land-proprietors derived great advantage from the employment of their Sokotelniki; and they unanimously determined to oppose the new regulation, as far as it related to themselves; they threatened to complain to the Porte through the channel of the Pashah of Widdin, who appeared willing to second their representations with all his influence. The ferocious Haffiz-Alli[22] had at that time the government of Widdin; and as he was the prince's personal enemy, he would have profited with eagerness of any opportunity to do him injury. The prince therefore modified the law relating to Sokotelniki, and those of the Bannat of Crayova were excluded from it. The following year he succeeded in compelling them to submit to a tax of twenty piasters each.

Another privileged class exists in both principalities, and is called *Poslujniki*; its number, however, is far inferior, and it is composed of some of the foreign peasants who come from Bulgaria, Servia, and Transylvania, to settle in the principalities.

The Poslujniki are given to the Greek Boyars, and to foreign residents of distinction; a custom which has become habitual since upwards of fifty years. They pay no money to the persons to whom they are attached; but it is their business to supply them with provisions of wood, barley, hay, poultry, eggs, butter, and game, in consideration of which they are exempted from government imposts, and receive some protection from their chiefs when they experience any vexations from the Ispravniks, or their subalterns.

Constantine Mavrocordato did not include the gypsies in the abolition of slavery; we shall place our remarks on this curious people in a more appropriate chapter.

At the last peace concluded at Bukorest between Russia and the Porte, it was stipulated that, in consideration of the two principalities having borne all the weight of the war, they should not, during the first two years after the day of their restitution, pay any tribute. The agreement was in the sequel merely observed with regard to the lood-system, through which it had been always customary before the war to collect the imposts; and, under a variety of other forms and denominations, contributions were paid to the Ottoman authorities of an amount proportionable to the present rates.

The most important regular revenues of the princes, after the *loods*, are derived from, the following branches:—

	PIASTERS.
In Wallachia, the salt mines, which annually give	600,000
The Vamma, or Customs,	380,000
The Port-Establishment	420,000
The Vinaritt, or tax upon wine; Oyaritt, or tax upon sheep; Dismaritt, or tax upon swine and bees; and a tax upon cattle feeding upon heaths and commons without licence	1,330,000

Total	2,730,000
In Moldavia their annual amount is 1,400,000 piasters.	

The administration of these branches of government is always sold to private speculators; and the above-specified sums have been paid by them in advance the last six years. Some merchants, and others possessed of considerable fortunes in the country, have acquired their riches by these speculations.

In Wallachia it has become customary that most of the public officers give a share of their profits to the prince, who, according to the estimate of their amount, receives it in anticipation; the whole together, with the value of the presents made to him on conferring titles of nobility, secure to him a private income of about two millions of piasters.

The metropolitan dignity, and all other sees, are in his gift. The former is usually granted for life, or for the time of the giver's reign. Its revenues amount to four hundred thousand piasters. They are derived from landed property bequeathed to the metropoly by deceased boyars and others, and from an annual capitation tax of fifteen piasters levied on the priests of the lower order, whose number amounts to fifteen thousand. The claims of the prince on this important revenue are not so openly avowed as on the civil offices; but they are understood with the person who is raised to the situation, or is confirmed in it by the successor.

The bishops of Argis, Rimnik, and Buzéo, are the next ecclesiastical dignitaries in rank, and the only qualified candidates for the metropoly among their numerous colleagues. They reside at Bukorest, and they form the supreme council of the church under the presidency of the archbishop. This council is the most corrupted tribunal of any in the country, and its acts and decisions, which proceed from any motives than those of moral tendency, would seem calculated for no other purpose than the encouragement of profligacy, and other disorders in the society. The will of the metropolitan, or that of the prince, is the only rule by which its concerns are conducted.

The constitution of Moldavia does not permit the prince to interfere with the affairs of the ecclesiastical council, nor with the financial concerns of the metropoly. The archbishop is elected by the nobility, and must be a native. The bishop of Romano, next in rank, is usually chosen to that dignity. The same regulations ought to exist in Wallachia, but a series of abuses have there rendered many evils irremediable.

Both principalities abound with monasteries originally established by different Voïvodes, and it was a long time customary with the inhabitants to consider as great acts of piety bequests of lands, houses, shops, or sums of money, made to them, insomuch that hardly any rich man died without having allotted a portion of his property to such a purpose.

These voluntary gifts had so accumulated, and the value of land has so increased, that some of the monasteries are now the richest establishments in the country. The greater number are in the gift of the reigning princes, who let them out for a space of time to the highest bidders. Others, being dedicated to the patriarchs of Constantinople and Jerusalem, are disposed of by them; but although the princes cannot appropriate to their own profit any part of their revenues, as they have the right of imposing taxes on them upon certain occasions, they frequently put them under contribution.

Besides the various important branches of revenue hitherto specified, the reigning princes possess many other means of raising money. The two principalities are an inexhaustible source of riches to them, and their proverbial appellation of 'Peru of the Greeks' is verified by experience.

CHAPTER IV.
GOLD AND SILVER MINES, &c.—PRODUCTIONS.—RESTRICTIONS ON THEIR EXPORTATION.—NAVIGATION OF THE DANUBE.—TRADE OF IMPORTATION.

The chain of Carpathian mountains which separates the two principalities from the Austrian dominions, abounds in a variety of minerals. Gold, silver, quicksilver, iron, copper, pitch, sulphur, and coals, are to be traced in many places; but although there is strong reason to believe they exist in abundance, no attempt is made to render them available, and this neglect is attributed to various motives, some of which would appear sufficiently justifiable.[23] The inhabitants maintain, that to undertake a work of a similar magnitude, the employment of a considerable capital and of a great number of men would be requisite, and consequently the country would have to support many heavy burthens long before it would begin to reap any advantage from their intended object; and that even after consenting to any necessary sacrifices, as the fruits of them would only serve to benefit the coffers of the Grand Signior, it is thought prudent to abstain altogether from creating so powerful an attraction to the leaders of the system of rapacity already too prevalent in the country.

On another hand, it is supposed that the precarious position of the Greek Hospodars, who live under the incessant apprehension of sudden recall and disgrace, induces them to bestow their whole attention to such resources only as are most immediately within their reach, and to neglect any plan that merely offers a remote prospect of gain.

The Porte then seems to be the only party much interested in this affair, as the only one capable of setting it properly on foot, and reaping a lasting advantage. Yet the Turks evince the same indifference, and political reasons are given in explanation, which, however, are by no means satisfactory; for surely no such considerations could prevent them from availing themselves of treasures which they have certainly assumed in every way the right of calling their own.

From all these conjectures, however, this conclusion can be drawn,—that as long as the principalities remain under Turkish influence, their mineralogic riches will be buried in obscurity and oblivion. The rivers Dimbovitza and Argis, taking their sources in the Carpathians, and crossing Wallachia to fall into the Danube, carry along a considerable quantity of grains of gold. The gypsies that belong to government are employed in picking them out of the sand when the waters are low; and they are allowed to pay their tribute partly from the fruits of this labour.

The trade of Wallachia and Moldavia, notwithstanding that it labours under a variety of restrictions and partial prohibitions, is one of their most important sources of opulence. Its details are little known, and less noticed beyond the neighbouring countries, although they are by no means deserving of inattention.

Of the common productions of the soil, the most abundant is wheat, of which the two principalities are supposed to give an annual return of ten millions of killows,[24] although hardly one-sixth part of their extensive and fertile plains is cultivated, and that a certain space of this is sown by Indian corn, barley, and hemp.

The other productions, proportionably important in a commercial point of view, are the bees-wax, honey, butter, cheese, hides, timber, staves, and ship-masts of all sizes and descriptions; and an annual supply of five hundred thousand hare-skins, six hundred thousand okes[25] of yellow-berries, and forty thousand kintals[26] of sheep's wool.

The three last-mentioned articles are alone perfectly free of exportation; the remainder are kept at the disposal of the Turkish government; and it is only in times of abundance, after the usual supplies have been fixed upon for the granaries and arsenal of Constantinople, that leave can be obtained to employ in foreign trade any portion of them. The exportation of wheat alone is considered as under a permanent prohibition; it is not in the power of the Hospodars to suffer any of it to be taken out of the country on private speculation; they must be authorised so to do by Ferman, a permit which is never granted to Rayahs, and very seldom to other Europeans, as the foreign ministers accredited at the Porte, aware of the difficulty of obtaining it, and the value that the Ottoman government would set in the gift of it, prefer abstaining altogether from applications on the subject, more especially as their success would only be profitable to some individuals, without being productive of any permanent good to the trade at large.

The quality of the Wallachian wheat is inferior, but it is far from being bad; that of Moldavia is better, and not differing much from the Polish wheat. Their ordinary price stands between 2 and 2½ piasters per killow. As an article of general trade, the charges upon it from the Danube to Constantinople, would hardly amount to one piaster more. The Turkish government send their own ships every year to transport their share of it, which is each time fixed at 1,500,000 killows, as well as the other articles necessary to their use, the quantity of which is not fixed, though generally very considerable.

The Moldavian timber is far better than that of Wallachia; it is of the finest oak, and perfectly well calculated for the construction of vessels. A great number of ships in the Turkish fleet are built of it, and fitted out with masts and ropes of Moldavian growth and origin. In the two provinces, these articles are sold at the lowest possible prices, and indeed the same thing may be said of all the prohibited articles; which, restricted as they are, from the monopoly arrogated by the Porte, have but little demand, except for the local consumption.

The hare-skins commonly stand at 35 paras[27] each, in large purchases, and the yellow-berries may be had at 40 or 45 paras per oke. The usual method of securing any quantity of these two articles at the lowest prices, is by bespeaking them at the different villages, and paying something in advance; the villagers engaged in such contracts never fail to fulfil them in proper time.

The hare-skins are of the first quality, but the yellow-berries are inferior to those of Smyrna, and only demanded when the crops in Asia Minor have proved deficient.

The sheep's wool is considered to be very good: cleaned and washed, it is sold at about 60 paras per oke, or 66 piasters per kintal, when in its original state, it is offered at 35 to 40 paras.

The principalities abound also in cattle and poultry of all descriptions. Every year they supply Constantinople with 250,000 sheep, and 3000 horses. They send, besides, a great number of these, and oxen, into the surrounding provinces, where they are usually sold at great profit.

All the productions and commodities that are employed for the exigencies of the Ottoman capital, are bought by the local government for about one-fourth of the prices current in the market, and one-sixth of their value in Turkey. They are paid for by a deduction from the common tribute, and, sometimes, by an extraordinary imposition of an amount equal to their cost.

Before we proceed to any remarks on the import trade, it is necessary we should say a few words on the town and harbour of Galatz, which may be called the seaport of the two principalities.

Galatz is in Moldavia, but nearly touches the frontier of Wallachia: it is situated at the beginning of the broadest and deepest part of the Danube, distant sixty miles from the Black Sea, sixty-five from Yassi, and seventy-two from Bukorest. The river is so far very navigable for ships not exceeding three hundred tons burthen. Its principal entrance from the sea is not very easy to make, owing to the islands which divide it into three great channels, two of which are very shallow and dangerous. But ships bound hither take pilots on board, and with this precaution, very few accidents take place, particularly in the fine season.

The navigation of the Danube closes in the month of November; and in the severest winters, even this part of the river is completely frozen over for the space of five or six weeks. In the month of March, ships begin to make their appearance again, and as they have not the inconveniency of a tide against them, they are enabled to come up close to the wharfs, and to remain there until their business is finished.

Galatz is the great market for the produce of the two principalities, and the only landing-place for some principal articles of importation. Having all the resources of a seaport, it is apparently a very flourishing town. Its market is always well stocked with the productions of the interior. The timber, masts, and staves are conveyed to it along the small rivers, that come from various parts of the country, and fall into the Danube nearest to it. There are public granaries for the wheat, and a great number of large warehouses, belonging to private merchants, for all articles. It is chiefly inhabited by commercial men, who, notwithstanding the rigour of the prohibitive measures, often find the means of exporting some quantity of wheat, and other contraband articles; but their principal trade is that of importation. The town and its dependencies are governed by two deputies of the Prince of Moldavia, called *Percalabi*. The number of the fixed inhabitants does not exceed seven thousand, but the great concourse of people occasioned every year by commercial pursuits, gives it the appearance of being very populous, and all the bustle of a place of great trade. The presence, in particular, of a great number of commercial vessels, increases considerably that appearance.

Although Galatz is the general *dépôt* for many goods of importation, it is not the principal market for them: they are conveyed to those of Bukorest and Yassi. Coffee, sugar, pepper, rum, lemons, oranges, and foreign wines, are the principal articles of this description. The local consumption of the first, in both provinces, is calculated at 800,000 okes every year; of the second, 900,000 okes; and of the third 35,000 okes; that of the others is merely eventual. Their importation, however, surpasses this quantity, and might be still carried to a greater extent, as the provinces of Galicia, Boukovina, Transylvania, Temesvar, and Servia are partly supplied with those articles by the markets of Bukorest, Yassi, and Galatz.

The general system of this import trade is ill contrived, and it is subject to many inconveniencies. The purchasers have recourse to the markets of Smyrna and Constantinople, where, of course, they buy at high prices. The goods, which have already paid custom-house duty in Turkey, are taxed with a new duty of the same kind, of three per cent., on being landed or brought into the principalities, as well as with other charges of an arbitrary nature, which amount to as much more. The latter are not, indeed, established by the local governments, but merely exacted by their officers, and as they are tolerated, they become unavoidable, unless the proprietors of the goods happen to be subjects of European courts, and as such, receive protection and assistance from the consuls residing in the country.

Wallachia and Moldavia are at present supplied by Germany with all kinds of cotton and woollen manufactures and hardware, either by land or by the Danube.

The plain and printed calicoes, the chintz, glass and earthenware, brought to their markets, are, without exception, German; but they are called English, and as such sold at higher prices than they would fetch were their origin made known.

The consumption of the woollen cloths is very extensive; that of the superfine qualities alone is valued at 200,000*l.* sterling every year. Some French cloths are brought into the country, but as their prices are considerably higher than those of Germany, they do not meet with much demand. French cambrics and English muslins are always profitable articles to speculators, and never remain long on hand.

As furs of all kinds form a part of the national costume, and are, besides necessary, owing to the natural rigour of the climate, they are an article of vast importation. Russia supplies the principalities with it, and takes in return brandy and wine, and imperial ducats.

Most of the merchants carrying on trade in these countries, are natives, or Greeks. Some have been naturalised in Russia or in Austria, and receive protection from those powers; an advantage which is of no small consequence to their affairs. Of late years, some natives of the Ionian islands have began to trade in the principalities, and the English flag, borne by their vessels, is now frequently displayed on the Danube.

Some overland expeditions of goods coming from Smyrna, are now and then made by way of Enos and Adrianople; but they are attended with risk and difficulty; besides which, the amount of charges surpasses by eight per cent. those incurred by way of Galatz.

The natural richness, and the various resources of Wallachia and Moldavia, are such, that if those countries could enjoy the important advantages of a regular government and a wise administration, under which industry and agriculture should receive their due encouragement, the trade of exports laid open, the commercial intercourse with foreign nations set upon a proper footing, and finally, the mines explored, they would in a short time become the most populous and most flourishing provinces of Europe. The harbour of Galatz would soon stand in rivalship with all the ports of the Black Sea, not excepting Odessa.

The fertility of the soil is such as to procure nourishment for ten times the number of the present population, and leave wherewith to supply other countries besides; the common return of cultivation being sixteen-fold, and in more favourable seasons, twenty-five.

Nature has furnished them with every possible means of becoming prosperous; men have ever proved themselves the determined enemies of their prosperity.

CHAPTER V.
BUKOREST AND TIRGOVIST, THE CAPITALS OF WALLACHIA.—YASSI, THE CAPITAL OF MOLDAVIA.—A DESCRIPTION OF THEM.—MODE OF TRAVELLING.—BREED OF HORSES.

Bukorest, the present capital of Wallachia, is an extensive dirty town, situated on a low and marshy ground, and containing eighty thousand inhabitants, three hundred and sixty-six churches, twenty monasteries, and thirty large *hanns* or caravanserays.

About four hundred years back it was but a small village, belonging to a person called *Bukor*, from whom it derived its name, and retains it to the present day. By degrees it became a town, and it continued increasing, until it surpassed the former capital, Tirgovist, in size. The Voïvode, Constantine Bessarabba, made it in 1698, the permanent seat of government; abandoning with all his nobles the city of Tirgovist, most delightfully situated further in the interior, having on one side a beautiful range of hills, and the other a very fine and extensive plain.

The Greek princes having continued to reside at Bukorest, probably on account of its being nearer to the Turks, Tirgovist was by degrees deserted by the remaining part of its inhabitants, and it is now reduced to a mere village. It contains many ruins of ancient edifices, amongst which those of the Voïvodes' palace are the most conspicuous. The river Dimbovitza runs alongside of it.

Yassi, the capital of Moldavia, is a smaller but better-built town, containing many elegant houses built in the most modern style of European architecture, forty thousand inhabitants, and seventy churches. One part of it stands upon a fine hill, and the other is situated in a valley. The prince's palace is the most extensive edifice in the whole town, and is surrounded by gardens and yards. It is furnished in a style which is half Oriental and half European, and has room enough to lodge conveniently more than a thousand people.

The palace of Bukorest was formerly a large building, standing on an eminence at one extremity of the town, and commanding a full view of it. In 1813 it was accidentally burnt down, and it has not been rebuilt. The late prince had, since that time, resided in two private houses joined into one.

Both capitals occupy a great extent of ground, the houses being separate from each other, and surrounded by yards or gardens, and trees. All the buildings are made of brick, and their walls, outside as well as within, are plastered and whitewashed. Tiles are seldom used, and the roofs are generally covered with wood.

The streets of the two capitals, and indeed of all the provincial towns, are, without exception, paved with thick pieces of timber, thrown across, and made tight to each other. In some, the surface is made smooth and even, whilst in others, the logs of wood are almost left in their natural state. In the rainy seasons they are constantly covered over with a deep liquid mud, and in the summer, with a thick black dust, which the least wind renders excessively injurious to the eyes and lungs; besides these great inconveniences, a complete renewal, at least once in every six years, is absolutely necessary.

At Bukorest, under the wooden pavements, to which the natives give the more appropriate name of *bridges*, there are large kennels, which receive the filth of the houses, and are meant to convey it to the river Dimbovitza, which runs through the town. Hardly any care is taken to keep the different passages open, and the accumulation of dirty substances frequently stops them up; in this state they sometimes remain for months in the hot season, during which they produce the most noxious exhalations, and occasion fevers of a putrid and malignant nature,—diseases to which the natural position of the town must alone dispose a great part of the inhabitants.

It has been long supposed, and it is still considered impossible to pave the streets with stone, not so much on account of the scarcity of the material, as owing to the ground being of a soft clay, which offers no hold to it. This idea, very prevalent among the natives, is certainly erroneous, and there cannot exist a more convincing proof of it, than the stone pavements constructed by Trajan and the Romans, which have so firmly withstood the destructive hand of time.

From a certain distance, and on elevated ground, the city of Bukorest offers itself to the view with great advantage; the mixture of the houses and trees give it a peculiar beauty; but it is like the fine scenery of a theatre which charms the distant eye, and on being approached is found to be a coarse daub.

As late as thirty years back, the Boyars were in the habit of visiting each other, and going to court on horseback, and the women of the most opulent only, went in coaches. Within that period, the fashion of riding in coaches has so increased, and it is now so universal, that no person of either sex, who has claims to respectability, can pass the gates of his house otherwise than in a coach, even in the finest weather. The Boyars consider it derogatory to their dignity to make use of their legs, and leave to the mob the vulgar practice of walking. The consequence is, that the streets, about seven or eight yards wide, are always full of carriages, and frequent accidents happen to the unfortunate pedestrians.

The kind of carriage most in use, is the German calèche; and the Boyars have introduced the fashion of having theirs ornamented in the most gaudy manner; but as they do not so much regard the beauty of the horses and harness, nor the dress of the coachman, it is very common to meet in the streets a carriage glittering with gold, drawn by a pair of miserable hacks, and driven by a gypsy in rags.

There are many coachmakers, both at Bukorest and at Yassi; but the carriages sent from Vienna are preferred to theirs, and much higher prices are paid for them. The Boyars are indifferent as to their solidity, and buy any old vehicle that is made up to deceive the eye, and is offered as new; fine ornaments being the only quality in estimation, every twelve or eighteen months they are obliged to purchase a new carriage. On another hand, their own inattention, and the lazy, slovenly, and careless habits of their coachmen, render this annual expense indispensable.

No coaches of any kind are to be hired, so that travellers, and other non-residents, must submit to the necessity of going on foot. Private lodgings are also seldom to be had, and it was but very lately that a public hotel was set up at Bukorest, which, being well furnished, and provided with every requisite commodity, has become very useful to travellers. A German is the proprietor and director of it.

The mode of travelling in the two principalities is so expeditious, that in this respect it is not equalled in any other country. Their post establishments are well organized; there are post-houses in all directions, and they are abundantly provided with horses. Every idea of comfort must, however, be set aside by those who are willing to conform themselves to the common method of riding post. A kind of a vehicle is given, which is not unlike a very small crate for earthenware, fastened to four small wheels, by the means of wooden pegs, and altogether not higher than a common wheel-barrow. It is filled with straw, and the traveller sits in the middle of it, keeping the upper part of his body in an erect posture, and finding great difficulty to cram his legs within. Four horses are attached to it by cords, which form the whole harness; and, driven by one postilion on horseback, they set off at full speed, and neither stop nor slacken their pace, until they reach the next post-house. Within the distance of half a mile from it, the postilion gives warning of his approach by a repeated and great cracking of his whip, so that, by the time of arrival, another cart is got ready to receive the traveller.

The Boyars, and other people of respectability in the country, travel in their own carriages, and at their own pace. In winter, as the snow lies about two months on the ground, sledges are generally used, as well in town as in the country.

The Wallachian breed of horses is of a peculiar kind. Their stature is very small, and they have no spirit; but they are strong, active, and capable of enduring great fatigue. Those of Moldavia differ only in being a little larger in size. Some of the richest people have their horses sent them from Russia and Hungary; but they are merely meant for their coaches, as, from an aversion to every exercise that occasions the least fatigue, hardly any of them ride on horseback. Handsome saddle-horses, consequently, are seldom seen in the country; the prince is the only person who keeps any; but they are chiefly used by his Albanians, or body-guard.

CHAPTER VI.
OBSERVATIONS ON THE GREEKS IN GENERAL.—THEIR INTRODUCTION TO THE PRINCIPALITIES.—THEIR POLITICAL SYSTEM.—CAUSE OF THE DECLARATION OF WAR BETWEEN TURKEY, RUSSIA, AND ENGLAND IN 1806.—THOSE WHICH OCCASIONED THE FAILURE OF THE ENGLISH EXPEDITION TO CONSTANTINOPLE.—SUBSEQUENT CHANGES OF POLICY OF THE OTTOMAN GOVERNMENT.—PEACE WITH ENGLAND.—PEACE WITH RUSSIA, AND CIRCUMSTANCES WHICH MOSTLY CONTRIBUTED TO IT.—HOSPODARS CALLIMACKI AND CARADJA.—PRINCE DEMETRIUS MOUROUSI'S DEATH.—CARADJA'S FLIGHT FROM WALLACHIA.—REFLECTIONS ON THE CONDUCT OF THE PORTE RELATIVE TO THE TWO PRINCIPALITIES.

None of the events that had influenced the political existence, and undermined the public spirit of the Wallachian and Moldavian nations, proved more ruinous to them than the system of policy introduced by the Greeks of the Fannar[28], when they were placed at the head of the principalities.

Humiliated, degraded, and oppressed as the Greeks were, since they had ceased to be a nation, civilisation degenerated among them, in proportion to the weight and barbarism of the yoke that had been imposed on them, and they had insensibly contracted those habits of corruption, and servile obedience, which must be inseparable from a state of slavery similar to theirs. Dissimulation and falsehood became the most prominent features of their character; and, in short, the force of the causes which acted upon them incessantly, familiarised them, by degrees, to every thing that could be degrading and humiliating to man.

The ambition of certain Greeks, leading an obscure life at Constantinople, was, however roused, when the office of state-interpreter at the Porte, assumed an important appearance under the direction of their countryman, Alexander Mavrocordato, who, from a petty merchant at the island of Scio, rose by degrees to that station, and was sent in the quality of Ottoman plenipotentiary to the congress of Carlowitz, where he distinguished himself as an able negotiator. He caused his son Nicholas to be raised to the governments of Moldavia and Wallachia, and he suggested to the Porte a new mode of appointment to those principalities, after the elective right had been entirely set aside. The Ottoman court thenceforward appropriated those two dignities to individuals who had once served in the quality of state-interpreter to its satisfaction, not so much as a reward for their services, as on account of the knowledge obtained of their personal character and extent of abilities.

On another hand, the repeated demonstrations of servitude on the part of the Greeks, and the apparent impossibility of their ever becoming a nation again, seemed to render them the fittest tools of the Porte's new system of government in the principalities; for, although it could not trample upon the whole of their privileges at once, yet, in giving them princes who should be entirely devoted to its interests, and slaves to its will, the existence of those privileges was rendered nugatory.

No sooner was the possibility of sharing in the public administration manifested to the Greeks, than such as were versed in the Turkish and European languages, abandoning all other pursuits, formed themselves into a distinct class, which assumed the title of nobility, and the exclusive right of being called to the service of the state.

In a short time, however, the number of competitors increased considerably; all equally eager and impatient to reach the same objects, they introduced a system of intrigue and bribery, which gave rise to continual changes in the government of the principalities, and accustomed the Porte to look upon these as farms which were to be let out to the highest bidders; the farmer-princes were therefore deposed and recalled, whenever the offers and promises of others of their countrymen appeared more advantageous.

From the period at which this system was introduced, to the beginning of the present century, being a space of ninety years, Wallachia alone has passed through the hands of forty different princes, independently of the time it was occupied by the Russians, from 1770 to 1774; by the Austrians and Russians, from 1789 to 1792, and by the Russians again, from 1806 to 1812.

The evils which naturally arose from such a state of things, weighed so heavily upon the two nations, that the court of Russia, already authorised by the treaty of Kaïnargik[29], to interfere in their behalf, insisted at the peace of Yassi in 1792, that the Porte should engage to maintain the princes of Moldavia and Wallachia in their respective stations, for the space of seven years, and not to molest them in any manner previous to the expiration of that term. This agreement was then legally entered into by the Ottoman plenipotentiaries, but in the sequel it was not regularly observed by the Porte, whose frequent infractions of it became the subject of continual remonstrance on the part of the court of Russia. In 1802, however, Prince Ipsilanti was appointed to the government of Wallachia, and Prince Alexander Mourousi to that of Moldavia, with the express condition which was obtained through the negotiations of the Russian minister at the Porte, that neither of them should be removed from office previous to the term stipulated in the treaty, if they were not proved guilty of an offence that the

Russian minister should allow to be of a nature which justified their deposition.[30]

In 1805, the intrigues of Buonaparte, who sought to involve Turkey in his continental system, prevailed upon the Porte to adopt a line of conduct which Russia could not otherwise interpret, than as a systematic violation of its existing engagements, and an approaching alliance with France, notwithstanding that a public audience of the Sultan was given to the Russian envoy, Mr. d'Italinsky, in which a formal exchange of ratifications took place of a late treaty of defensive alliance concluded between the two powers.

The Hospodars, Ipsilanti and Mourousi, were suddenly recalled, without the participation of the Russian embassy; the latter was replaced by Charles Callimacki, and the former by Alexander Sutzo, a man who was looked upon as a partisan of Buonaparte, and who had always been obnoxious to the interests of Russia.

Previous to this circumstance, a certain degree of coolness already existed between the courts of St. Petersburgh and Constantinople; it originated in the Porte's sudden resolution of suppressing foreign protections, in abolishing all letters-patent, until then granted to individuals, natives of Turkey, who were authorised by such letters to place themselves under the protection of foreign courts, although residing and trading in the Ottoman dominions. More particularly in carrying that resolution into effect, by forcibly and publicly compelling all such individuals, protected by Russia, to give up their titles, without paying the least regard to the representations of the Russian embassy.

Ipsilanti's and Mourousi's deposition brought things to a crisis. A Russian army was immediately sent to the frontiers to enforce the treaties, and having occupied the fortresses of Bender and Hotim, the Porte looked upon the measure as a declaration of war, and the Mufti issued his *Fetvaa*[31], which declared it legal to repel force by force.

The rupture was soon followed by another with England, who had joined Russia to oppose the increasing influence of Buonaparte over the Porte. When, in 1805, the English ambassador, Mr. Charles Arbuthnot, arrived at Constantinople, the Porte expressed a wish of renewing the treaty of accession made in 1799, the term of which (eight years) was drawing to its end. That treaty, framed upon the wisest principles, completed the triple alliance between England, Russia, and Turkey, from which so many important advantages have accrued to the common cause.

Mr. Arbuthnot not being invested with full powers for that particular object, wrote home for instructions, and received them a short time after; and when on their arrival an offer was made to the Turkish ministers to commence the work, they very unexpectedly began to draw back, and an actual recantation took place, which naturally created the greatest surprise.

The intrigues of the French ambassador, and Buonaparte's progressive encroachments in Europe, had made on the minds of the Sultan and his ministers such an impression, that no remonstrance, no threat could now induce them to perform what they themselves had shown so much wish for before.

On the other hand, the British embassy could not remain indifferent to the recall of the Hospodars, and to the manner in which the foreign protections had been suppressed.

From an impulse of official regard to the complaints and interests of those individuals who were patentees under the English protection, and in consequence of the Russian envoy's solicitations that their efforts might be joined for the purpose of resisting the violent measures pursued by the Turkish government, the British ambassador made many representations to the Porte against its proceedings, and although impartial in principle as to the practice of granting protection to natives of the country, he, at all events, recommended moderation, and a less offensive mode of carrying the new system into execution. But having soon discovered and ascertained beyond a doubt, that all interference was of no avail, that the resolution of the Turkish cabinet was such as to hazard all, sooner than withdraw from the adopted plan, he deemed it expedient to advise the British patentees to proceed, as if from their own accord, and give up their titles to the Porte, and in the mean time recommended in a private manner, the property and personal safety of such individuals, who, by this means, not only avoided the resentment of the Turkish government, but were all well treated, and some taken into favour.

The British ambassador, however, showed less disposition to compliance with regard to the other proceedings of the Porte, and having insisted with Russia on the immediate reinstatement of the Hospodars Ipsilanti and Mourousi, the subject was discussed at the divan, where the general opinion inclined to a firm resistance of those pretensions; but the Sultan finally declared, that however humiliating might be the alternative of ceding to them, he was resolved to recur to it rather than break with England.

This decision was at the time carried into execution, to the extreme disappointment of the French ambassador, Sebastiani, whose great object was to kindle the fire he had raised. But very soon after, advices being received that the Russian troops had already entered the Moldavian territory, affairs underwent a total change; the Russian envoy was dismissed, and the Grand Vezier took the field.

To represent these events in a more proper point of view, it is necessary to observe, that it was neither the intention of England, nor the wish of Russia, to engage in a serious war with Turkey. Their object was to bring the Porte to a sense of its true interests, in diverting it from a line of conduct which bore every appearance of a change in its political system, and was every way calculated to confirm the suspicion that the Sultan was contracting an alliance with Buonaparte.

In order to separate the Porte from the French party, and induce it to return to the connexions which had formerly existed with the allies of Turkey, a plan of coercive measures had been found necessary; and, to give them a greater weight, it had been determined that Russia should send an army from the north, and England a fleet from the south.

When the English fleet appeared before Constantinople, it naturally occasioned the greatest confusion and alarm. The Sultan lost no time in sending on board to offer terms of peace, and negotiations were commenced with Mr. Arbuthnot, who was in the flag-ship, the Royal Sovereign. But they were carried on with much less vigour than it was necessary to give them, and left time to the French intrigues to gain the advantage. Buonaparte's active agents, General Sebastiani and Franchini[32], were the more anxious to counteract the operations of the English plenipotentiary, as they were aware that the first result of his success would have been the expulsion of the French embassy from Constantinople. They employed for that purpose every means in their power, and they succeeded by the following stratagem.

The chief of the Janissaries, Pehlivan-Aga, had formerly been colonel of a regiment, which had acted once as guard of honour, given to a French embassy at the Porte. Having remained some time in that station, he had contracted a lasting connexion with the French, to whose party, since that period, he devoted himself. When General Sebastiani saw that peace with England was on the point of being concluded, he sent Franchini to him to suggest a plan which the Turkish officer carried into immediate execution. He went to the seraglio[33], as if in great haste, and having obtained audience of the Sultan, he thus addressed his imperial chief:—

"May God preserve your sacred person and the Ottoman empire from every possible evil. A pure sense of duty brings me before your Royal Person, to represent that so strong and general a fermentation has arisen amongst my Janissaries since the appearance of the infidel's fleet before your royal palace: they express so great a discontent at the measures pursued by your ministers in negotiating with the English, from a shameful fear that the appearance of that fleet has thrown them into; that a general insurrection is on the point of breaking out, unless the negotiations be laid aside, and all offers of peace be rejected with scorn. They declare that it is beneath the dignity and fame of the Ottoman empire, to submit to such an act of humiliation, as to sign a treaty, because a few ships have come to bully its capital, and dictate their own terms to the Ottoman sovereign. Your brave Janissaries will not suffer so disgraceful a stain to tarnish the splendour of the Ottoman arms. They are all ready to sacrifice themselves in defence of your residence, and in vindication of the honour and faith of the Ottoman nation. But they can never consent to stand tacit witnesses of a submission so ignominious to the Turkish name."

Sultan Selim, a prince naturally timid and credulous, no sooner heard a message of this sort delivered in the name of the Janissaries, then in good understanding with the chiefs of government, and apparently united with the troops of the Nisam-y-gedid[34], than he ordered all communications with the English fleet to be suspended, and immediate preparations of defence to be made, in the event of its commencing hostilities.

This manœuvre, unknown at the time, and with which very few persons are yet acquainted, was the true cause of the failure of the negotiations which, at the commencement, bore so sure a prospect of success.

The fleet returned without even having made a show of hostile intentions, and left to the triumphant French party the most decided influence in the Seraglio.

Before we enter into further observations on the events which followed, it may not be amiss to make a few remarks on the character of those who were then at the head of the Turkish administration, as it is to them that the whole change of system of the Porte is to be attributed.

Haffiz-Ismaïl Pashah, Grand Vezier, appointed early in 1805, was a low-bred, ignorant man, so poor and thirsty after money, that the moment he was elevated to his station, he formed the plan of operating a change in the principalities of Wallachia and Moldavia, although the time prescribed by the treaties was not yet near, with a view of getting a subsidy, and securing to himself an income which the candidates, who took no small advantage of the Vezier's inexperience and selfish views, had promised to allow him when the appointment should have taken place.

Ibraïm-Aga, Kiaya-Béÿ, or minister of the interior, a man of little experience and great ambition, under the idea of ingratiating himself with his master, and rendering, as he thought, a signal service to the state, undertook the affair of protections which he treated in a manner so insulting and provoking, that it was impossible for any foreign power, jealous of its own dignity, to suffer it to remain unnoticed.

The Mufti, Sheriff-Zaadé-Attaa-Effendi, and the chief of the Janissaries, Pehlivan-Mehmet Aga, were entirely devoted to the French party. They willingly seconded the adoption of any measures which tended to alienate the Porte from England and Russia, and appeared calculated to promote Buonaparte's scheme of overthrowing the triple alliance.

Galib Reïs-Effendi, minister of foreign affairs, and Yussuf-Aga, Validay-Kiayassi or chancellor to the Emperor's mother, were the only two men in power friendly to the common cause. They disapproved of the measures pursued, but their opinion was over-ruled, and they both thought it prudent to retire from business, in order to screen themselves from responsibility with respect to the consequences they foresaw.

The military operations on the Danube be between the Russians and the Turks, which followed the first acts of hostility, were not more successful with regard to the object that brought them on, than the threats of the English fleet.

The peace of Tilsit took place; and the Porte, which had reason to expect an effective interference on the part of Buonaparte in behalf of its differences with Russia, gained no other advantage than the conclusion of a long armistice, the first condition of which was the retreat of the Russian armies from the principalities, whence, however, they did not remove. Negotiations for peace were, notwithstanding, set on foot; and the great revolutions, which overthrew the Sultan Selim, and consigned him to death, finally established a new order of things at Constantinople, and operated a complete change in the political system of the Turkish cabinet. The Porte remained no longer blind to the equivocal conduct of Buonaparte since his reconciliation with Russia, and began to look upon its state of hostility with England not only as useless, but even injurious to the interests of the country.

In 1808, an English[35]plenipotentiary had been for the second time[36] sent to treat at the Dardanelles, and peace was definitively signed in the month of December of the same year.

At the same time the Turkish plenipotentiaries, sent to Bukorest during the armistice, were endeavouring to adjust the differences with Russia; but the interview of the Emperor Alexander with Buonaparte took place at Erfurth, and the failure of their joint proposals to the court of London[37] was followed by instructions to Prince Prosoroffsky, commander-in-chief of the Russian armies in Moldavia and Wallachia, to signify to the Ottoman plenipotentiaries that, as the Emperor Alexander had acceded to the Continental System, the chief object of which was a continual state of warfare with England, he could no longer enter upon terms of peace with Turkey, unless the English ambassador, lately admitted at Constantinople, were sent out of the Ottoman dominions.

The Turkish ministers expressed astonishment at the versatility of the court of Russia, which, having made the first overtures for a negotiation, had not then in any manner alluded to England; they demanded time, however, for the arrival of instructions which were necessary to regulate their official reply to a communication so unexpected. They dispatched a messenger to Constantinople for that purpose, and he was accompanied by an aide-de-camp of Prince Prosoroffsky, Colonel Bock, who, on his arrival, signified to the Porte the Emperor's ultimatum, through the channel of the French minister Latour Maubourg.

The Ottoman government, without much hesitation, recalled the Turkish plenipotentiaries from the congress of Bukorest, and hostilities were renewed.

A plan of partition had been formed at Erfurth between the emperors Alexander and Napoleon, by which the Turkish provinces were to fall to the share of Russia, and Spain to that of France. It was after this understanding between the two sovereigns that overtures were made to England. The English negotiation took time, and before it came to a decided issue, Buonaparte declared to his senate that the principalities of Wallachia and Moldavia were annexed to the dominions of his friend and ally the Emperor Alexander. When, however, Buonaparte found England determined to treat upon no basis which did not expressly admit of the evacuation of Spain, and that by entering into such terms he left a decided advantage to Russia with respect to Turkey, without reaping any benefit to himself from the political bargain made at Erfurth, he changed his views. The continental system, which he endeavoured to justify in attributing the general calamities of Europe to a tyrannical perseverance in war on the part of England, furnished him with a sufficient pretext for engaging Russia to continue her war against Turkey, who had just entered into terms of friendship with England. On the other hand, he prevailed upon the Turkish government to insist on the restitution of the principalities occupied by the Russian armies, and to continue hostilities so long as the Russian court should withhold its consent to that measure. His desire of keeping these two powers at variance with each other could not but increase when he had subsequently formed the plan of invading Russia, who, molested on one side by the Turks, and on the other by the Persians, was thus forced to employ considerable armies on distant frontiers.

The exhausted state of Turkey, the mediation of England, and the impatience of Russia, who was pressed by the hostile preparations of France, evidently intended against her, hastened the conclusion of peace in 1812 between the Mussulman powers and the Russians; but, critical as the circumstances were, the Court of St. Petersburgh signed a most advantageous treaty with both.

Galib Effendi, who, since the great changes of government at Constantinople, had resumed the functions of minister of foreign affairs, was chief plenipotentiary at the congress of Bukorest in 1811 and 1812; but the Greek prince Demetrius Mourousi, who, in his quality of state-interpreter, was present at the negotiations, conducted the greatest part of them, and was indeed intrusted with extensive power. He had, with his two brothers, been invariably attached to the Russian party since the beginning of his public career, and his hopes of being appointed to one of the principalities, the greatest objects of his ambition, after the restoration of peace, appeared grounded upon the best foundation. His office, his services at the congress, and the support of the court of Russia, were, in fact, considerations which appeared to render his nomination certain.

The cession of Wallachia and Moldavia could not, therefore, by any means, suit his views, and he combated it with energy and success; but, in rendering so important a service to the Porte, some proof of attachment to Russia was also necessary on his part; and although by insisting on the entire restitution of the principalities, no doubt but the Russian plenipotentiaries, who were instructed to hasten the conclusion of peace upon any terms not beyond that restitution, would have consented without hesitation, Mourousi, who was aware of it, finally settled the conditions by ceding to Russia the finest part of Moldavia, that which is situated between the rivers Dniester and Pruth, thus fixing the future line of demarcation of the Russian frontiers by the direction of the latter river.

The vigilant agents of Buonaparte at Constantinople did not suffer the conduct of Mourousi to remain unnoticed. When, after the signing of the treaty, they saw themselves frustrated in the hope of inducing the Porte to continue the war, they sought to bring the Mourousi family into disgrace, that they might, at least, prevail upon the Ottoman government to place at the head of the principalities persons of their own choosing. They represented the Prince Demetrius as a traitor who had been bribed by the Russians to serve their interests, at a time when it was in his power to obtain the most advantageous terms of peace.

Meanwhile hostilities commenced between France and Russia, and the Porte having evinced a resolution of remaining neutral, unwilling to give umbrage to either of the contending powers in the choice of the new Hospodars, resolved to fix upon two individuals whose political principles had never been connected with foreign parties. A great number of candidates offered their services, but none of them being qualified for the appointments, their claims were rejected. Halett-Effendi, intimate counsellor of the sultan, was instructed to make a choice, and he fixed it on the prince Charles Callimacki[38] for Moldavia, and Yanco Caradja for Wallachia. Halett-Effendi had been several years before Turkish secretary to Callimacki's father, whilst at the head of the Moldavian government, and on terms of intimate friendship with Caradja, who had also a subaltern employment under the same prince. Being perfectly acquainted with the personal character of both, he recommended them to the sultan as the fittest persons in those circumstances, and they were appointed in August 1812.

Demetrius Mourousi, who, with Galib Effendi, had not yet departed from Wallachia, received the news of the nominations at a time that he expected with confidence that of his own. He was at the same time secretly informed that his return to Constantinople would expose him to the greatest dangers, and advised to retire into a Christian country. Offers were made him of an asylum in Russia, with a considerable pension from the government; but, fearful that his flight might direct the vengeance of the Porte on his family, who had remained in the power of the Turks, and in the hope of justifying his conduct, since the whole responsibility of the transactions at the congress ought properly to have fallen on Galib Effendi, he made up his mind to accompany that minister back to the capital. He little suspected, however, that the Turkish minister, whose conduct had been disapproved of, had removed every unfavourable impression relative to himself from the mind of the Sultan, by attributing the conditions of peace to which he had subscribed, to the intrigues and treachery of Mourousi; and that he had, in consequence, received secret orders to arrest the Greek prince the moment they crossed the Danube together, and send him prisoner to the Grand Vezier, who had not yet removed his head-quarters from Shumla.

Mourousi, still more encouraged by the friendly assurances of Galib Effendi, left Bukorest in September, and from Rustehiuk was conveyed under an escort to Shumla, where, on entering the gates of the Vezier's dwelling, he was met by several Chiaoushes[39] who fell upon him with their sabres and cut him in pieces. His head was sent to Constantinople, where it was exposed three days at the gates of the Seraglio, with that of his brother Panayotti Mourousi, who, during the absence of Demetrius had filled his place at the Porte, and was accused of having been his accomplice in betraying the Ottoman interests.

The Hospodars Caradja and Callimacki took possession of their respective governments on the 3d of October, 1812, the day fixed for the restitution of the principalities; and the Porte, whose present security on the side of Russia, in a great measure depends on the strictest adherence to its treaties with that power, has made no attempt of removing the princes previous to the expiration of the seven years.

The Hospodar Caradja, however, having in the course of six years' residence in Wallachia, amassed immense wealth, apprehensive of being called to account on his return to Constantinople for laying aside so many riches for his own use, judged it prudent to make a timely retreat, and to settle in some Christian country of Europe beyond the reach of Turkish influence. He remitted all his money to European banks, and one day in October, 1818, he assembled some of the principal Boyars, consigned to them the reins of government, and left Bukorest with all his family for Kronstadt in the Austrian dominions, where he arrived in safety after a short journey.[40]

After his departure, the Boyars petitioned the Sultan that he would no longer appoint Greek princes to govern Wallachia, but confide the administration to the members of the divan, who engaged to accept and maintain any tributary conditions that he would think proper to prescribe to them. The Ottoman cabinet, however, did not conceive it prudent to listen to the proposal; and after communicating with the Russian ambassador, appointed to the principality the same Alexander Sutzo, who had been so strongly opposed by the Russian Envoy in 1805.

Russia had no longer reasons to object to his nomination; and no doubt but the Prince Sutzo, who is an enlightened and well-thinking statesman, will acquit himself of his charge as well as the circumstances in which he is situated, will permit. But the harassing and ruinous system of government, still maintained in the principalities, offers, it must be confessed, no small matter of regret on the indifference of the Porte with regard to the adoption of measures better calculated for their welfare and prosperity.

The Ottoman court has often witnessed the consequences of the dread with which the Greeks employed in its service are impressed, and has felt on various occasions how much its policy must tend to alienate from the Turks every sentiment of good-will of the inhabitants of those provinces, and make them desirous and ready to throw themselves into the arms of the first nation whose armies approach their territory to make war on Turkey; and yet it continues in the same system. Greek princes, however devoted to the interests of the Porte, would certainly do little without armies, in the event of an unexpected revolution in Wallachia and Moldavia. Their presence alone is by no means sufficient to maintain in them the Turkish authority. The fortified places on the Danube, are the only guarantees of the fidelity of the principalities. In suffering the two nations to be governed entirely by their own natural authorities, would the Ottoman supremacy incur the least diminution of power? and would it not continue to maintain the same commanding advantages?

The inattention of the Turkish cabinet is not to be exclusively ascribed to the general system of governing the empire, but chiefly to the selfish views and personal avidity of the ministers who compose it. They have accustomed themselves to look upon Wallachia and Moldavia as two rich provinces over which they have but a momentary authority; and, instead of seeking the means most calculated to secure a permanent possession of them, they shorten the possibility by a systematic devastation of all their resources.

The Sultan himself, who takes a much more active part in the affairs of state than many of his predecessors have done; whose talents and liberal sentiments would claim equality with those of any other sovereign, were they not so much restrained by the religious prejudices and stubborn ignorance of his Mahometan subjects: and whose chief attention has of late years been directed to a new organization of the empire, unfortunately seems equally averse to any changes which might tend to improve the condition of Wallachia and Moldavia.

CHAPTER VII.
CLIMATE.—ITS INFLUENCE.—EDUCATION OF THE BOYARS.—SCHOOLS.—WALLACHIAN TONGUE.—MODERN GREEK.—NATIONAL DRESS, MUSIC, AND DANCE.—AMUSEMENTS.—HOLIDAYS.—MANNERS OF SOCIETY.—MARRIAGES.—DIVORCES.—RELIGION AND SUPERSTITION.—AUTHORITY OF THE CHURCH.—ITS INDEPENDENCE OF THE PATRIARCHAL CHURCH OF CONSTANTINOPLE.

The proximity of the Black Sea and of Mount Hæmus on one side, and that of the Carpathian Mountains on the other, render the climate of the principalities variable, and subject to sudden changes from heat to cold.

When the wind comes from the north-east, even in the middle of summer, it cools the atmosphere to such a degree, as to force the inhabitants to cover themselves with additional clothing. The southerly wind brings heat and fine weather; but it seldom lasts any length of time.

A great quantity of rain falls during the summer, and in the months of June and July it is always accompanied by storms of wind and thunder, which regularly return every day at the same hour towards the evening.

The winter is almost always long and tedious, and the summer heats set in all at once at the beginning of May, so that the beauties of a regular spring are little seen or known.

The severest part of the winter begins early in December, and the same degree of cold, with little variation, lasts until the middle of February, when a damp and unhealthy temperature succeeds, and continues until May. The Danube and all the rivers that fall into it from the principalities generally remain frozen for six weeks, and the ice is thick enough to bear with perfect safety the heaviest artillery. The snow lies on the ground the whole of January and February, and communications with every part of the country are carried on with sledges.

From the latter part of September to the middle, and frequently to the end of, November, the days are the finest in the year. But the nights are excessively cold, and the night air particularly unwholesome. Travellers who do not take care to guard against its influence by flannels and thick clothing, are exposed to the danger of various kinds of fevers, and of the pleurisy.

The irregularity of climate, the damp quality of the soil, and an abundance of marshy places throughout the principalities, produce a visible influence over the animals of the various sorts which are common to them, as well as over the vegetation. The bears, wolves, and foxes, are of the most timid nature;

hardly any danger is to be apprehended from them, unless they are met in numerous flocks, as is common enough during the coldest winter nights.

The domestic animals are also remarkable for mildness. The beef, pork, mutton, poultry, and game, have rather an insipid taste; the vegetables an inferior flavour, and the flowers little perfume.

Finally, man, the chief work of nature, is here of a dull and heavy disposition: with weak passions, no strength of mind, and betraying a natural aversion to a life of industry or of mental exertion. Moral causes may indeed produce such effects upon the human frame; but here, those of a physical kind evidently act in unison with them, and with equal force.

The education of the Boyars is usually confined to the mere knowledge of reading and writing the language of the country, and the modern Greek. Some few add to this superficial stock of learning, a few of the rudiments of the French language, which has been introduced by the Russian officers among them. Many more understand and speak it without the least knowledge of its letters or grammar. If any are able to talk familiarly, though imperfectly, of one or two ancient or celebrated authors, or make a few bad verses that will rhyme, they assume the title of literati and poets, and they are looked upon by their astonished countrymen as endowed with superior genius and abilities. An early propensity to learning and literature receives but little encouragement; and, at a more advanced period in life, the allurements of public employment, the petty intrigues at court, and the absence of every obstacle to pursuits of gallantry and pleasure, induce even the best disposed to set aside every other occupation.

Public schools have, since several years, been established both at Bukorest and Yassi. They are supported at public expense, and attended by masters for the Wallachian, ancient and modern Greek languages, writing, and arithmetic. The number of students at each school amounts at the present moment to about two hundred. They are the sons of inferior Boyars and tradesmen. The children of the principal Boyars receive their education at home from private tutors, commonly Greek priests, who are not natives of the principalities.

The education of the women is not more carefully attended to than that of the men; sometimes it is inferior, on account of the prevailing custom of marrying them at a very early age.

Neither sex is regularly instructed in religion, and it is by the mere intercourse of life that they derive their notions of it, and by the examples of their elders that their principles in it are regulated.

These circumstances, naturally arising from the discouragement given by the government to every improvement in civilisation, keep the state of society very backward, and are productive of the most pernicious influence over its moral character.

The Boyars, indeed, although so little susceptible of great virtues, cannot be taxed with a determined propensity to vice. Established prejudices, which the general state of ignorance has rooted in the two nations, and a universal system of moral corruption, render them, however, familiar with it.

Money is their only stimulus; and the means they generally employ to obtain it are not the efforts of industry, nor are they modified by any scruples of conscience. Habit has made them spoliators; and in a country where actions of an ignominious nature are even encouraged, and those of rapacity looked upon as mere proofs of dexterity and cunning, corruption of principles cannot fail to become universal.

The prodigality of the Boyars is equal to their avidity; ostentation governs them in one manner, and avarice in another. They are careless of their private affairs, and, with the exception of a few more prudent than the generality, they leave them in the greatest disorder. Averse to the trouble of conducting their pecuniary concerns, they entrust them to the hands of stewards, who take good care to enrich themselves at their expense, and to their great detriment. Many have more debts than the value of their whole property is sufficient to pay; but their personal credit is not injured by them, neither do they experience one moment's anxiety for such a state of ruin.

The quality of nobility protects them from the pursuits of the creditor; and the hope of obtaining lucrative employments, by the revenues of which they may be able to mend their affairs, sets their minds at ease, and induces them to continue in extravagance. Some bring forward their ruin as a pretext for soliciting frequent employment, and when the creditors have so often applied to the prince as to oblige him to interfere, they represent that the payment of their debts depends upon his placing them in office. The office is finally obtained, and the debts remain unpaid. When a sequester is laid upon their property, they contrive to prove that it came to them by marriage; and as the law respects dowries, they save it from public sale.

The Wallachian or Moldavian language is composed of a corrupt mixture of foreign words, materially altered from their original orthography and pronunciation. Its groundwork is Latin and Slavonic. For many centuries it had no letters, and the Slavonic characters were used in public instruments and epitaphs. The Boyars, whose public career rendered the knowledge of a few letters most necessary, knew merely enough to sign their names. The Bible was only known by reputation. In 1735, Constantine Mavrocordato,who had undertaken the task of replacing barbarism by civilisation in both principalities, made a grammar for the jargon that was spoken, in characters which he drew from the Slavonic and the Greek. He caused several copies of the Old and New Testament in the new language to be distributed, and he ordered the Gospel to be regularly read in the churches. He encouraged the inhabitants to study their language according to the rules of his grammar, and in a few years the knowledge of reading and writing became general among the higher orders.[41]

The modern Greek, introduced by the Hospodars, is the language of the court, but it is perfectly understood by the Boyars, with whom it has become a native tongue. It is spoken in Wallachia with much greater purity than in any other country where it is in use. In many parts of Greece, different dialects have been adopted, some of which have but little affinity with the Hellenic, whilst in others the greater part of the words have been so disfigured as to render their origin difficult to trace. The Greek spoken in Wallachia differs but little from the Hellenic. The Moldavians are less in the habit of making use of it; and the study of French and other foreign languages is more general among them.

The national dress of the Boyars does not differ from that which belongs to the higher classes of Turks, with the only exception of the turban, to which they substitute a kind of cap of an extraordinary size called *calpack*, made of grey Astracan fur, in the shape of a pear. It is hollow, and the largest part of it is about three feet in circumference, with a proportionable height. It is altogether a very ugly and ridiculous head-dress, and not at all adapted to the beauty and magnificence of the rest of the costume.

The ladies dress entirely in the European style; but they combine the fashions with oriental richness and profusion of ornament. Their persons, in general, have not much beauty; but this deficiency is made up by a great share of natural grace and pleasant humour, and by a peculiar neatness of shape.

The Wallachian music has some resemblance with that of the modern Greeks, although more regular in time, and altogether more harmonious. Its style has hardly any variety, and all the tunes are uniformly played in minor keys. Some would produce good effect if played with proper delicacy and expression. The instruments mostly used are the common violin, the Pan-pipe, and a kind of guitar or lute peculiar to the country. The bands are composed of these three kinds of instruments, all of which play the leading part without variation of accompaniment; they are only introduced on occasions of mirth or festivity. The Boyars, being no admirers of music, never make a study of it, and their gypsy slaves are the only persons who profess it. Their women, however, are partial to the German style of it, and several of them perform on the pianoforte; but want of perseverance keeps them from reaching to any degree of perfection, and want of emulation from persevering.

The dance, formerly common to all the classes of the natives, and which, at present, is the only one known to the lower orders, is of a singular style. Fifteen or twenty persons of both sexes take each other by the hands, and, forming a large circle, they turn round and round again, at a very slow pace; the men bending their knees now and then, as if to mark the time of music, and casting a languishing look on each side, when holding the hands of women. This kind of dance has some years since been thrown out of fashion in the first circles of society, and English country-dances, waltzing, and the Polish mazurka have been introduced. Most of the ladies dance them well, but the men very indifferently, their dress being a great obstacle to perfection in the accomplishment.

In the daily occupations and pastimes of the Boyars, little variety takes place. Those who hold no place under government, spend their leisure in absolute idleness, or in visiting each other to kill time. In Wallachia, the management of their estates and other private concerns, which do not relate to public appointment, does not occupy much of their attention, and sometimes the finest of their lands are left in total neglect, or in the hands of mercenary agents, who enrich themselves with their spoils. They hardly ever visit their country possessions, which some let out for several years, for much less than their real value, when they find customers who are willing to pay the whole amount of rent in advance. They build fine country-houses which they intend never to inhabit, and which, in a few years, fall into ruin. The most delightful spots in their beautiful country have no power to attract them, neither is it at all customary with them to quit the town residence at any season of the year.

The Boyars in Moldavia, like those in Wallachia, are the great land-proprietors; but they bestow much more of their attention and time to the improvement of their estates, which they make their principal source of riches. The revenues of some of the most opulent, from landed property, amount to two or three hundred thousand piasters, and their appointment to public employment is generally unsolicited.

During the winter, the chief amusements of the Boyars at Bukorest consist in attending public clubs, established on the plan of the *redoutes* at Vienna. Masked balls are given in them three or four times a week, which attract great numbers of people. There are, however, clubs adapted to the different ranks; the principal of them, to which the court and first Boyars subscribe, is distinguished by the appellation of *Club-noble*; it is very numerously attended towards the end of the Carnival, and although its title indicates a perfect selection of society, it does not the less allow entrance to people of all descriptions under masks. The most genteel do not dance here, unless they are masked; but they play at the pharao-table, and at other games, of which the place offers a variety.

Private balls are also given sometimes, but no other kind of regular evening parties are customary. Formalities of invitation, however, are never expected; and the tables of the Boyars, and their houses, are at all times open to their friends and acquaintance.

The summer evenings are generally spent at a place called *Hellesteo*. It is a lake situated about a mile's distance out of town, on the borders of which, the company walk or sit two or three hours. Near the most frequented part is a coffee-house, where ices and other refreshments are to be had. On Sundays, the number of carriages coming to this place, amounts sometimes to six or seven hundred; and the multitude of fashionables, as well as the great display of dress and jewels of the ladies, certainly render it a gay and pretty scene. The walks are not shaded by trees, and the only advantage they offer, is an extensive view round the country.

At the distance of a mile from the *Hellesteo*, is situated a beautiful little grove called *Banessa*, to which a part of the company frequently drive. It is the property of a Boyar of the name of Vakaresko, and forms a kind of park to his country-house, situated behind it. This gentleman is not only good enough to keep it open to the public, but even makes every possible improvement for their accommodation, at his own expense. Both he and his lady do the honours of it to their friends, in the most obliging manner.

All the company return to town from these places at the same time; the line of calèches, endless to the sight, raise clouds of dust, to the no small derangement of the ladies' toilets. Some spend the remainder of the evening in riding up and down the principal streets, and others assemble at different houses to play at cards.

In winter, the afternoon rides are confined to the streets of the town, where the number and splendour of sledges is equal to that of the calèches in the fine season.

Last year a company of German actors came to Bukorest, and after some performances, were encouraged to establish a regular theatre. They gave German operas, and comedies translated into Wallachian, and the first two or three months they attracted crowds from all the classes, who, without exception, seemed to have taken a true liking to the new sort of amusement; but latterly the charm of novelty had begun to wear off, and the Boyars of the first order, with some of the principal foreign residents, seemed to be the only persons disposed to support the continuance of the establishment, more with the view of making it a place of general union of the society, than from the attractions of the stage.

The days of Christmas, new-year, the prince's anniversary, Easter, and some others, are chiefly devoted to etiquette visits at court. From nine o'clock in the morning to one in the afternoon, the prince and princess, seated at the corner of a very long sopha, and covered with jewels and the most costly apparel, receive the homage of all those who are entitled to the honour of kissing their hands, an honour which the foreign consuls, their wives, and officers attached to their suite, alone, think proper to dispense with. No other persons residing in the country can be received at court on gala days without going through that formality. The wives of Boyars are allowed to sit in the presence of the prince and princess; they take seat according to the rank or office of their husbands, who without exception are obliged to stand at a respectful distance. On similar occasions, the crowd at court is immense; the whole of the outer apartments are filled with persons of every description, and the audience-chamber is not less so by the number of visitors. On new-year's-day it is customary to make presents of money to the servants attending the court; they have no other pecuniary allowance for their services; and the bustle and confusion occasioned by the avidity of this crowd of harpies is as difficult to be described as it is inconsistent with the dignity of a court who expects and ordains universal homage to its chiefs.

About two hundred and ten days of the year are holidays, and they are strictly observed by the inhabitants, as far, at least, as relates to the exclusion of all kinds of work. The public offices, although they have so great a portion of the year to remain inactive, are allowed, besides, a fortnight's vacation at Easter and during the hottest days of summer. In these useless and pernicious days of idleness, whilst the Boyars' chief occupation consists in seeking the means of killing time out of their homes, the lowest classes spend it with their earnings at the brandy-shops, where prostitutes are kept for the purpose of attracting a greater number of customers, and of propagating with vice the most horrible of all the diseases with which human nature is afflicted.

The number of this disgraceful class of females is so great at Bukorest, that the late Aga, or police director, suggested to the prince the plan of levying a capitation tax on each, whereby he would create a new revenue of some hundred thousand piasters. This plan, contrary to expectation, was not put into effect, though it was not likely to meet with obstacles.

The manners of society among the Wallachian Boyars are not remarkable for refinement. The general topics of social conversation are of the most trivial nature, and subjects of an indecent kind frequently take the place of more becoming discourse; they are seldom discouraged by scruples of any ladies present.

In the habitual state of inaction, brought on by a natural aversion to every serious occupation which does not immediately relate to personal interest, both sexes, enjoying the most extensive freedom of intercourse with each other, are easily led to clandestine connexion; the matrimonial faith has become merely nominal.

Various other customs contribute to the domestic disorders prevailing in a great number of private families. Parents never marry their daughters, to whatever class they may belong, without allowing them dowries beyond the proportion of their own means, and to the great detriment of their male children, who, finding themselves unprovided for, look upon marriage as the means of securing a fortune, and consequently regard it as a mere matter of pecuniary speculation. Feelings of affection or sentiments of esteem are therefore out of the question in the pursuit of matrimonial engagements, and money remains the only object in view.

When a girl has reached the age of thirteen or fourteen, her parents become anxious to procure a husband for her. They do not wait for proposals, but make the first offers, sometimes to three or four men at a time, stating with them the amount and nature of the dowry they are disposed to give. They enter into a regular negotiation when a greater amount is required, and finally settle with him who remains satisfied with the most reasonable terms. The inclinations of their daughter are never consulted on the occasion, and too great a disparity of age, or other personal defects on the part of the future husband, never appear to them objectionable. The girl is sometimes perfectly unacquainted with the man of her parents' choice; and, at her tender age, unable to form any judgment on the state of matrimony, she submits to their will with indifference. Not long after the nuptials, she is left perfect mistress of her actions, her domestic affairs are entirely put into the hands of the servants, and she never interferes with them. Neglected by her husband, and at full liberty to dispose of her time as she thinks proper, she forms connexions of intimacy with women more experienced in the world than herself. The attractions of pleasure and society become too strong to be resisted, and the example of others, with the numerous temptations that surround her, prove, sooner or later, fatal to her virtue. To the harmony which may have subsisted between her and her husband, succeeds disgust; quarrels soon follow, and blows sometimes are not spared on her. Her condition becomes at last intolerable, she quits her husband's house, sues for a divorce, and generally obtains it, however frivolous the plea in the true sense of the law. Her fortune is given back to her, and enables her to live single, or to attract another husband, if she feels again an inclination to matrimony. She is now allowed her own choice of one; but, once accustomed to the agreeable paths of diversity, she seldom remains more faithful to the second than she had been to the first.

The church of Wallachia and Moldavia is the only one professing the Greek religion that authorises divorce; or more properly speaking, the only one that abuses the power of pronouncing it, the authority being granted to the patriarch of Constantinople on occasions of the most particular nature, and indeed never made use of.

In the principalities, the sentence of divorce is pronounced so frequently, the motives alleged are sometimes so frivolous, that it never affects the reputation of a woman, so as to degrade her in her ordinary rank of society; nor does it in the least become a scruple to the delicacy of the men, whatever may have been the nature of its motive.

There are but few families at Bukorest who have long continued in an uninterrupted state of domestic harmony, and fewer still who can point out some relation who has not gone through a divorce.

Sometime back, a Wallachian lady of quality, who had brought but a small fortune to her husband, became desirous of fixing her residence in one of the principal streets of the town, and she pressed him to lay aside his accustomed system of economy, to sell his estate, the revenue of which gave them the principal means of support, and to build a fine house in that street. The husband, more reasonable than herself, positively refused to listen to her extravagant proposal; and the lady, incensed at his upbraiding her for it, quitted his house, and shortly after sued for divorce, which she obtained. This lady, who has since remained single, professed great piety, and is still considered as a very pious woman.

Not long after, a young Boyar, contrary to custom, fell in love with a very beautiful young woman, of the same rank and age. The parents of both agreed on their union, and the nuptials were celebrated by public festivities. This couple was looked upon as the only one in the country whom a strong and mutual attachment had united. At the end of the first year the husband was suddenly attacked by a pulmonary complaint, and induced by the physicians' advice to separate himself for some time from his wife, and go to Vienna in order to consult the best medical men. After eighteen months' absence, finding himself perfectly recovered, he hastened back to Bukorest impatient to see his wife, to whom he had not ceased to write, but whose letters had latterly become much less frequent. On his arrival he found the most unexpected changes in his family affairs. His wife had gone to her parents, refused to see him, and had already consented to marry another! Her father, who was the chief instigator of her sudden resolution, had negotiated the second marriage, because it suited his own interests.

The legitimate husband claimed his spouse through every possible channel; but he was not listened to, and government declined interfering.

The sentence of divorce was pronounced by the metropolitan; and, although the husband's refusal to sign the act rendered it perfectly illegal, the second marriage took place; the ceremony was performed by the archbishop in person, and public rejoicings were made on the occasion.

The circumstances of this adventure were the more remarkable, as the second husband had been married before, and divorced his wife after six weeks' cohabitation, when he saw the possibility of obtaining this lady's hand.

Another lady of the first rank separated her daughter from her husband, with whom she had lived six years, and caused a sentence of divorce to be pronounced. She gave for reason, that her daughter's constitution suffered considerably by frequent pregnancy. The husband, who was by no means inclined to the separation, and who knew his wife to enjoy the best health, made remonstrances to no effect: and he was condemned by government to give back the dowry, and to pay damages to a considerable amount, for having spent a part of it, although he proved to have employed the deficient sum for the use of his wife and family.

These three instances of the degraded state of morals in these countries are selected from numerous others that occur daily. They are such as to excite astonishment, and appear almost incredible; yet they created no other sensation at the time than other common news of the day, deserving but little notice.

It is customary in Wallachia for parents to interfere in their married children's family concerns, and to exercise nearly the same authority over them after marriage as before. They are often seen as busy in intriguing to bring on a separation, as they had been active in seeking husbands or wives for them.

The absurdities of superstition, which form so great a part of the fundamental principles of the present Greek faith, have gained equal strength in Wallachia and in Moldavia: even the most precise doctrines of the Christian religion are there corrupted by the misconceptions or selfish views of low-bred and ignorant priests, a set of men, indeed, who have here made themselves a manifest disgrace to the sanctity of the Christian name.

A celebrated writer has said that 'Climate has some influence over men; government a hundred times more, and religion still more.'[42] This observation is particularly applicable to these countries, and its truth illustrated by their present condition. Either of the two last-mentioned causes, separately, would have acted with force upon the morals of their inhabitants. Intimately connected as they are, the evils that result are most deplorable.

The mode of instructing the Wallachians and Moldavians in the precepts of religion, is not, however, calculated to animate them with excessive zeal and to propagate fanaticism. They are merely taught to plunge headlong into all the ridicules of superstition, the inseparable attendant of ignorance; and it is probably owing to the total absence of fanaticism that the priesthood exercise a less powerful influence here, than they do in other Greek countries. All the ecclesiastical dignitaries being of obscure origin, and mostly of the lowest extraction, they are personally despised by the Boyars. Their spiritual power is alone respected.

The rites ordained by the established church are the same as those of the patriarchal church. Persons who have not received baptism in it, are not considered as Christians, nor even honoured with the name of such.

Frequency of confession and communion, and the punctual observance of a vast number of fast-days, during the year, are prescribed with severity. They have become the most essential points of faith, and the people believe with confidence that an exact adherence to them is sufficient to expiate the heaviest crimes, particularly after the confessor's absolution, which, in most cases, is to be obtained by the means of a good fee.

Attending divine service at a very early hour on Sundays and other holidays, and three or four times a day during the week of the Passion, is also required and observed; the signs of devotion performed in it, consist in making crosses and prostrations before the images, kissing them, and lighting a candle to some favourite saint. The Gospel, when read, is heard with indifference and inattention. Preaching is not customary.

The laws of the church strictly forbid matrimony between persons who are in any degree related to each other: they even go so far as to prevent marriage between people whose parents may have stood godfathers to either in baptism. The severity of the matrimonial laws is still greater with respect to the difference of religion, when one of the parties belongs to the Greek church. A transgression would be followed by a sentence of divorce, and punished by excommunication, if the marriage, already concluded, were persisted in. The dread of this last evil is so great to all the natives, that every sacrifice is made in preference of being exposed to it.

The patriarch of Constantinople, although acknowledged as chief of the religion, has no controul over the church of the two principalities and exercises but little influence over its chief dignitaries.

CHAPTER VIII.
PEASANTS—THEIR MANNERS AND MODE OF LIVING.—
EMIGRATIONS.—AGRICULTURE.—GENERAL ASPECT OF
THE COUNTRY.—AN ACCOUNT OF THE GYPSIES.

There does not perhaps exist a people labouring under a greater degree of oppression from the effect of despotic power, and more heavily burthened with impositions and taxes, than the peasantry of Wallachia and Moldavia; nor any who would bear half their weight with the same patience and seeming resignation. Accustomed, however, to that state of servitude which to others might appear intolerable, they are unable to form hopes for a better condition; the habitual depression of their minds has become a sort of natural stupor and apathy, which render them equally indifferent to the enjoyments of life, and insensible to happiness, as to the pangs of anguish and affliction.

Hence it is in a great measure inferred that they are a quiet and harmless people. Their mode of living is, indeed, with regard to the intercourse among themselves, an uninterrupted calm. Although the male part are given to drinking, quarrels and fighting are almost unknown among them; and they are so much used to blows and all kinds of ill treatment from their superiors, that they approach with the greatest respect and submission any who bear upon themselves the least external mark of superiority.

Their religious notions, grounded upon the most ridiculous superstition, are extremely singular. They firmly believe in all sorts of witchcraft, in apparitions of the dead, in ghosts, and in all kinds of miracles performed by the images of saints, and by the virtues of the holy water. In illness, they place an image near them, and when they recover, though it were through the assistance of the ablest physician, they attribute their return to health to the good offices of the image alone. Their observance of Lent days is so strict, that the threats of instant death would hardly prevail upon any one to taste of the aliments specified in the endless catalogue of forbidden food. Their other Christian duties, although similar to those of the superior classes of their countrymen, are carried to greater excess. Invoking the Holy Virgin or any saint, is always substituted to regular prayer. Divine Providence is never directly addressed.

The villages throughout the country are principally composed of peasants' huts, all built in the same style and of the same size. The walls are of clay, and the roofs thatched with straw, neither of which are calculated to protect the lodgers from the inclemency of the bad seasons. The groundfloors are, however, occupied as long as the weather will permit, and in winter they retire to cells under ground, easily kept warm by means of a little fire made of dried dung and some branches of trees; which, at the same time, serves for cooking their scanty food. Each family, however numerous, sleeps in one of these subterraneous habitations, men, women, and children, all heaped up together; and their respective beds consist of one piece of coarse woollen cloth, which serves in the double capacity of matrass and covering.

Their ordinary food is composed of a kind of dough to which they give the name of *mammalinga*, made of the flour of Indian wheat, sometimes mixed with milk. The first two or three days after a long Lent, they sparingly indulge themselves in meat; but the greater part cannot afford even so great a treat, and content themselves with eggs fried in butter, and the milk to their mammalinga.

They continue the whole day out of doors at work, and they bear with indifference all the extremes of the weather. Their industry, however, is not of a very active kind, and they take frequent rest.

Notwithstanding this mode of life, and the supposed influence of an ungenial climate, the generality of the peasants are a fine race of people. They have no peculiar turn of features which may be called characteristic; from long intercourse with foreign nations, their blood seems to have become a mixture of many. The Eastern black eye and dark hair, the Russian blue eye and light hair, the Greek and Roman nose, and those features which distinguish the Tartars, are equally common amongst all the orders of these two nations.

Both sexes are in the habit of marrying very young. They are not given by inclination to sensual pleasures; but as religion does not teach the women the propriety of virtue, excessive poverty induces them to grant their favours for any pecuniary consideration, frequently with the knowledge and consent of their husbands, or parents.

In the holidays, they spend most of their time in the village wine-houses, where they eat and drink, and sometimes dance. At other times they enjoy the spectacle of bear-dancing, a very common amusement throughout the country, conducted by wandering gypsies, who teach the art to those animals while very young, and gain a living by exhibiting them afterwards.

The dress of the male peasants bears some resemblance to that of the Dacians, as represented in the figures of Trajan's pillar at Rome. Their feet are covered with sandals made of goat-skin. They wear a kind of loose pantaloon which is fastened to the waist by a tight leather belt, and closes from the knee downwards. The upper part of the garment is composed of a tight waistcoat, and a short jacket over it, of coarse cotton stuff, and in winter is added a white sheep-skin, which is hung over the shoulders in the manner of an hussar's pelisse. The head is not deprived of any part of its hair, which is twisted round behind, and a cap is used to cover it, also made of sheep-skin, but which in summer is exchanged for a large round hat. The beard is shaved, and the whiskers alone are left to their natural growth.

The women are clothed from the neck to the ancles with a long gown of thick cotton stuff of a light colour, made tight at the waist in such a manner as to render the whole shape visible. They generally go barefooted, and they cover their heads with a common handkerchief, merely meant to keep up the hair. On holidays they add to their common shift a coloured gown of a better sort: they button it up from the waist to the neck, round which they wear as ornament, one or more strings of beads, or *paras*, pierced through for the purpose.

Since their emancipation, the peasants have not been fixed to particular parts of the country, and they are at full liberty to change their habitations at the end of their engagements with the landholders. But those of a more respectable kind seldom quit the spots where chance has once placed them, unless they are driven by imperious circumstances.

Notwithstanding the unfortunate position of this people, by no means enviable to their neighbours, the miseries of famine in Transylvania sometimes cause considerable emigrations of peasants from that vast province into Wallachia and Moldavia. All the best lands in Transylvania being in the hands of Hungarians, Szecklers, and Saxons, the others who form the bulk of the population are driven into hilly and barren situations, where at all times they subsist with difficulty; and of late years the more than ordinary scarcity that prevailed has driven about twenty thousand peasants, subjects of the emperor, into the dominions of the Hospodars, where the great disproportion between the number of agricultural hands and the extent of arable land, renders such emigrations extremely useful. They are placed on the same footing as the native peasants with regard to tribute.

The changes of residence that sometimes take place among the peasantry are not detrimental to the collection of the imposts, as it is the business of the Ispravniks of each district to ascertain, every six months, the number and means of the individuals living within the limits of their Ispravnicates, and amenable to taxation. The deficiency of any particular district being made up by the increase in another, no loss accrues to the treasury.

There is no regular system exercised with respect to the arrangements of the landholders and peasants. In general, however, the latter are allowed a share of the produce in kind, with an understanding that the burthen of the taxes and impositions falls upon them; not that the former would be averse to taking upon themselves the payment of their tenants' contributions, but because government is decidedly against the introduction of a similar regulation, the amount and nature of the imposts being nominally fixed, but always exceeding the regular rates.

As the Boyars proprietors of land in Wallachia never cultivate the estates for their own account, but merely rent them to those who can make the greatest offer of ready money, the less valuable are sometimes given to the whole body of peasants, residing in them when the advances are made by them. The richest estates give an income of fifty or sixty thousand piasters: but they are divided and subdivided for marriage-portions for the proprietors' daughters; and if the custom continue for a few generations longer, a system, something similar to the agrarian law, must be the future consequence.

The manner of tilling the ground does not materially differ from that of other countries in Europe; oxen are employed instead of horses.

The wheat is sown during the Autumn; the barley and Indian corn in Spring. The harvest of the two first generally takes place in the month of July; that of the latter at the beginning of September; and as this article is required for the nourishment of so great a portion of the population as the peasantry, the quantity of it sown and reaped every year is equal to that of wheat. Barley being only made use of for feeding cattle and poultry, it is sown in a much smaller proportion.

The vine is always planted on the sloping of hills, and in situations where it can receive some protection against any sudden severities of the weather; the grape is seldom gathered before the end of September; and as it does not come to a perfect state of maturity, it makes but indifferent wine, of a light and sourish taste. All other kinds of fruit, common to Europe, come here in great abundance at their usual seasons.

The great waste of land left in both principalities in a state of nature, and the universal custom of not cultivating the immediate vicinity of the high roads, give to the country, in many parts, an appearance of desolation; and a traveller, who only judges by the scenery within his view, is apt sometimes to think himself in a wilderness; he meets with few habitations on his way, except those attached to the post-houses, and hardly perceives any other population.

But of all the sensations of delight produced by the beauties of nature, none can surpass that which is raised by the aspect of the more interior parts of this country. Romantic hills and dales, rivulets and streams, fields adorned with verdure and flowers, present themselves in a successive variety of beauty during the fine season, particularly within twenty or thirty miles of the Carpathians, from the Pruth to the Danube at Orsova. The inner parts of those mountains themselves offer the most magnificent scenery; and their summits, the most beautiful and extensive views. Those who have seen the romantic parts of the Alps, cannot help recalling them here to their remembrance; the impressions of the moment are such that they feel at a loss to decide which deserve the preference. Whilst the impatient courier, going over the rough roads through the Carpathians, bestows curses on the dangers that slacken his pace, and impede his progress, the voluntary traveller and lover of nature stands lost in admiration, and finally quits with reluctance and regret scenes which nature has formed in her most romantic mood.

The aspect of the Carpathians is very different in winter: all the heights are covered with snow, and the narrow roads with mud and large stones, rolled in the midst of them by the torrents, so as to render them almost impassable; mostly situated on the brinks of dreadful precipices, at the bottom of which rivers or torrents have formed their passage, one false step of the passenger is immediate death.

The Hospodars purposely neglect to repair these roads; the fear of creating suspicions at the Porte that they wish to facilitate the passage of foreign troops into the principalities, induces them to abstain from an undertaking, which in other respects has become so imperiously necessary: they do not even venture the slightest representation to the Porte on the subject.

Few peasants inhabit this part of the country; during the summer they cut down wood, and supply with it the inhabitants of the plains, who burn nothing else. The most stationary are attached to the post-houses, situated here and there for the purpose of assisting the necessary communications between the Austrian and Ottoman states. Their long residence in this neighbourhood is generally marked by the glandular accretion, common to the inhabitants of the Alps. It grows sometimes to an immense size; its appearance is then most disgusting, and it absorbs almost all the faculties, moral and physical, of the unfortunate beings afflicted with it. The natives believe the cause of this evil to proceed from the qualities of the snow-water always drunk by those who inhabit the mountains.

Every village throughout the country has a small church or chapel belonging to it, and one or more priests who act as curates. The ecclesiastics of this order are chosen amongst the ordinary peasants, from whom they are only distinguished in appearance by a long beard. They lead the same life, and follow the same avocations when not engaged in the exercise of their clerical functions; but they are exempted from the public imposts, and pay nothing more than their annual tribute of fifteen piasters to the metropolitan. The generality of them can neither read nor write; they learn the formule of the service by heart; and if a book is seen in their chapels, it is very seldom for use. The priests of this order are, in each district, dependent on the *Archimandrites*, or Vicars, of the parishes nearest to their abode.

That class of the human species comprehended under the general appellation of gypsies, seems to be, like the Jews, spread in most parts of Europe, and in many other parts of the world; like them having no admissible claims to any country as exclusively their own, and distinguished from the other races of men by physical and moral qualities peculiar to themselves. The different gradations of climate, and the state of civilisation of the countries in which they are born and brought up, do not seem to affect them in the same manner as the other classes of human nature, and in many respects they appear little superior to the brute creation.

Wallachia and Moldavia contain about one hundred and fifty thousand gypsies, and make a more profitable use of them than other countries do, by keeping them in a state of regular slavery. The period of their first coming there is not exactly ascertained; but there is every reason to believe it dates with the irruption of the gypsies from Germany in the fifteenth century; and they are mentioned in some manuscripts, possessed by Wallachian and Moldavian convents, evidently written towards that period.

They are remarkable, as every where else, for their brown complexion; their bodily constitution is strong, and they are so hardened from constant exposure to all the rigours of the weather, that they appear fit for any labour and fatigue; but their natural aversion to a life of industry is in general so great, that they prefer all the miseries of indigence, to the enjoyment of comforts that are to be reaped by persevering exertion. The propensity to stealing seems inherent in them, but they do not become thieves with the view of enriching themselves; their thefts never extend beyond trifles.

The women have the same complexion, with fine and regular features. They are very well shaped before they become mothers; but soon after they begin to have children, and they are generally very fruitful, their beauty gives way to a disgusting ugliness.

Both sexes are slovenly and dirty: the filth and vermin with which their bodies are infected, seem to form a necessary part of their existence, as no consideration can induce them to be cleanly. Most of them are clothed with a few rags, and their children go naked at almost all seasons.

They acknowledge no particular religion as their own; neither do they think of following the precepts of any, unless, acting as domestic slaves, they are ordered so to do by their masters. Among themselves they dispense with the religious ceremony of marriage, and although many live together as husbands and wives, they are only bound by the ties of nature.

The women are of the most depraved character: none of them follow the regular line of public prostitutes, but at the same time none refuse their favours when the slightest offer of money is made.

In both principalities the gypsies are divided into two distinct classes of slaves; the one is composed of those who are the property of government, and the other, of those who belong to private individuals. No regular traffic of them is carried on in the country, neither is it customary to expose to public inspection any who are to be disposed of. Both sales and purchases are conducted in private, and the usual price for one of either sex, is from five to six hundred piasters.

The number of gypsies belonging to the two governments, altogether amounts to eighty thousand, including women and children. They are suffered to stroll about the country, provided they bind themselves never to leave it, and to pay an annual tribute of the value of forty piasters each man, above the age of fifteen. We have mentioned on the subject of the gold and silver mines, how those of Wallachia pay their share of it.

They are dispersed in different parts of the principalities, living in separate companies of ten or fifteen families, under tents; they frequently change the place of their abode, keeping always in the neighbourhood of towns and villages, or near the high roads. A passenger coming in sight of their tents is always assailed for charity by a quantity of naked children belonging to them, and does not easily get rid of their importunities without throwing a few paras to them.

The chief occupation, both of the men and women, leading this vagrant life, consists in making common iron tools, baskets, and other wood-work of the kind for sale. But their industry and gain are confined to what is absolutely necessary for procuring them the means of subsistence. They possess a natural facility and quickness in acquiring the knowledge of arts; but a small number, however, devote themselves to any, and musical performance seems to be that to which they give the preference: those who profess it attend the wine-houses every day, for a trifling remuneration, and from thence they are frequently called to the houses of the first Boyars, on occasions when a band of music is requisite. Some few become masons, and receive one piaster for a whole day's work. They are always employed, with a number of their less experienced companions, in public buildings, and they are then allowed no other reward but their daily food, and a proportionable deduction from their tribute.

The other class of gypsies is divided into families belonging to Boyars and others, who select from among them the greater part of their household servants. The remainder are either employed at the vineyards of their masters, suffered to follow common trades, or allowed to wander about the country, upon the same conditions as those of the government.

The practice of employing gypsy slaves in various departments of the household, particularly in the kitchen, is universal in both principalities; but although the expense saved by it is considerable in houses where a great number of servants must be kept, the inconvenience is much greater, though not felt. The kitchens of the Boyars are, from the filthy habits of the cooks, and the inattention of the masters, not less disgusting than the common receptacles of swine. The incurable propensity to vice, and the laziness of these servants, occasion incessant trouble and vexation. Almost at every house punishments are instituted for them, the most severe of which is the bastinado applied to the naked soles of the feet: it is performed by another gypsy, under the inspection of the superintendent, and frequently under that of the master or mistress. The ladies of quality, however young and beautiful, do not show much delicate reluctance in similar instances of authority.

The secondary punishment consists in passing the culprit's head through a kind of iron helmet, with two immense horns of the same metal, and locking it under the chin in such a manner as to render it extremely troublesome to the bearer, and to prevent him from eating or drinking, as long as he keeps it on.

It is, however, certain, that the gypsy servants can neither be kept in proper order without punishment, nor be made to go through any long work without the stimulus of stripes. The private owners have not the power of death over them; but it has happened sometimes, that some unfortunate wretch has been beaten to death, and neither the government nor the public took notice of the circumstance.

It is under the care of these depraved servants, that the children of Boyars are brought up. The women of the higher ranks not being in the habit of nursing their infants, place them in the hands of gypsy wet-nurses, whose mode of life exposes them incessantly to diseases which must prove most prejudicial to the quality of their milk, and whose bad nourishment and dirty habits, must otherwise affect the constitution of the children.

Notwithstanding that the gypsies form here so necessary a part of the community, they are held in the greatest contempt by the other inhabitants, who, indeed, treat them little better than brutes; and the insulting epithet of 'thief,' or any equivalent, would sooner be put up with than that of 'gypsy.'

The public executioners for any kind of punishment are chosen from that class alone; but as their office is merely momentary, the unfortunate beings condemned always suffer considerably more from their inexperience and incapacity.

The Wallachian and Moldavian gypsies speak the language of the country; but those who lead a wandering life use, amongst themselves, a peculiar jargon composed of a corruption of Bulgarian, Servian, and Hungarian words, mixed with some Turkish. Its pronunciation, however, sounds so much like that of the Hungarian tongue, that a person accustomed to hear both without understanding either, is apt to mistake the one for the other.

Their quality of slaves is acknowledged by the surrounding nations; and those who abscond to them are restored when claimed as private property. Desertions, however, are not frequent; and when they do take place, the fugitives take such precautions as to prevent the place of their concealment being discovered.

CHAPTER IX.
INTERCOURSE OF FOREIGNERS.—FOREIGN CONSULS.—HOW FAR THE NATIVES ARE BENEFITED BY THEIR INTERCOURSE WITH FOREIGN RESIDENTS.

A considerable number of foreign Europeans reside in both principalities, where they are attracted by a variety of resources.

The principal merchants and bankers, either from birthright or from foreign naturalisation, carry on their business under the immediate protection of European courts; without which the general system of the local governments, so prejudicial to the interests of trade, would give but little security to their operations.

There are at both capitals several German and French coachmakers, carpenters, builders, architects, teachers of European languages and music, physicians, and apothecaries, all of whom have rendered themselves extremely useful to the native inhabitants, and derive no small profit from the exercise of their respective professions. Almost all the importers of foreign furniture, luxuries in ladies' apparel and other kinds of retail trade, undertakers of subscription-clubs, and of coffee-houses of the better sort, ladies' shoemakers, mantuamakers, and taylors, are also European foreigners.

A great number of Transylvanian and Hungarian gentry of the inferior rank are attracted by the advantages of renting the Boyars' estates. According to the treaties existing between the Porte and other powers, foreign subjects are not permitted in any manner to hold, as proprietors, landed property in the Ottoman dominions; the prince of Moldavia observing how little this stipulation had been attended to in his principality, thought it necessary, in 1815, to issue a decree which ordered the expulsion of foreign farmers. The Boyars, whose best estates were under their management, and who had every reason to be satisfied with them, strongly opposed the measure; their representations finally induced the prince to give his tacit consent to their wishes; and, properly speaking, this stipulation of the treaties does not include the principalities of Wallachia and Moldavia, and ought not to be applied to them.

The progress of the Russian arms previous to the peace of Kaïnargik, had enabled the cabinet of St. Petersburgh to become the arbiter of the fate of Turkey. Whatever might have been the Empress Catharine's motives for consenting to the conclusion of that peace, she did not remain less sanguine in her favourite project of conquering the empire of the East, and the special clauses in the treaty, which gave her the power of interfering in the affairs of the Wallachians and Moldavians, were calculated not only to secure to her the affections of the people for whom they were most immediately intended, but at the same time to incline the other Christian subjects of Turkey to look upon her as their natural defender, and their future deliverer.

No subsequent events prevented her from employing her right of interference, though, according to circumstances, it may at times have been exercised with more or less energy; and the policy pursued by her successors evidently denotes the continuation of a system which has an important object in view, however distant the possibility of attaining it.[43]

In order, however, to exercise her influence with the activity necessary to ensure success, the empress had insisted also that the Porte should acknowledge the residence in the two principalities of imperial agents, to whom she thought proper to give the title of consuls, as most adapted to screen her views, and to justify her apparent one of enlarging the trade of her empire, and giving protection and assistance to those of her subjects who were willing to extend their commercial transactions to the principalities. This pretext was in fact plausible; for the Russian merchants who had till then been in the habit of trading in those countries, had complained much of the difficulties and vexations they had constantly experienced from the irregularities of the local governments.

However unwilling to recognise the future residence of public agents from the court of Russia, the Porte was unable to oppose it with any prospect of success, and consequently consented.

The court of Vienna soon after followed the example, though from motives of a more commercial nature; and the consuls of Russia once admitted, the Ottoman government could not refuse to acknowledge those of Austria.

The Greeks saw with no little regret the arrival of these foreign agents, who not only checked their authority over the foreign trade, but became also competent witnesses of their political system and administration, and the accredited reporters of all their actions. But, as it was out of their power to oppose the arrangements of the imperial courts, they thought it best to set their submission to the profit of their vanity in receiving the consuls as envoys sent by foreign powers to independent princes. They introduced for their reception the formalities and ceremonial of the public audiences given by the Grand Vezier to European ambassadors at Constantinople, and they revived the custom of the Voïvodes, of being seated on an elevated throne on similar occasions.

Under the republic of France, French consuls were sent for the first time to reside in the principalities, and their establishment has been kept up without interruption under the successive governments of France. On several occasions they were very useful to Buonaparte.

A British consul-general was for the first time appointed in 1802 to reside at Bukorest, chiefly for the purpose of facilitating the overland communications between England and Turkey. After the peace of Tilsit he was recalled, and the consulate was renewed in 1813, with the additional motive of promoting commercial intercourse with the principalities.

The pope has for many years been represented by a bishop in Wallachia, and by a vicar in Moldavia; the latter has recently been promoted to the rank of a bishop.

The number of Roman Catholic inhabitants is considerable; most of the Servian, Bulgarian, and Transylvanian settlers belong to that persuasion. They have two fine churches at Bukorest and at Yassi.

There are also two protestant churches originally founded by Charles XII. of Sweden during his long residence in the principalities. They are superintended by a vicar appointed and paid by the archbishop of Stockholm. The protestant inhabitants are German, and their number amounts to one thousand. All foreign churches, provided they profess the doctrines of christianity, are not only tolerated in the principalities, but allowed a variety of privileges which they cannot enjoy in any part of the Turkish dominions. The metropolies seldom interfere with their affairs, and when any circumstance obliges them so to do, they bear every possible regard to their institutions, and never assume the tone of superiority.

In general, the social intercourse between the natives and foreign inhabitants is carried on upon a much more friendly footing than might be expected from the number of national prejudices that still divide them, in opinions, religion, and established customs. The natural hospitality of the Boyars makes no exceptions with foreigners; and if on one hand this quality loses a part of its merit in being the mere effect of custom, on the other it does not deserve the less credit when totally divested of ostentatious motives.

It would appear that little benefit is to be expected by the inhabitants of a country long occupied by Russian armies, and made the principal theatre of military operations. Yet the late intercourse between those of the principalities, and the Russians, and the prospect of their being incorporated with the Russian empire, have, in many respects, improved their civilisation. A variety of barbarous customs existing before have been abolished; usages and institutions were introduced which tended to their improvement, and the exterior manners of the Boyars have undergone a polish which is not unworthy of more enlightened nations. Those of Moldavia would view with pleasure any political change in their country which offered to them the sure prospect of improvement in civilisation. Those of Wallachia have long since consoled themselves for the improbability of any early change, by taking a very active part in the general system of rapacity, of which it has become the lot of their countrymen of inferior order to bear the weight.

GENERAL OBSERVATIONS
ON THE
POLITICAL POSITION OF THE PRINCIPALITIES.

When we reflect upon the deplorable condition of Wallachia and Moldavia, examine the causes of their evils, and cast an eye upon the numerous gifts with which nature has enriched them,—when we compare the effects of demoralisation and ruin, which are the natural consequences of their present system of administration, to the advantages that would accrue to them from a regular and permanent form of government,—it is hardly possible not to regret that the question of a change in their political fate was not proposed and resolved at the late congress of Vienna.

A variety of facts related in the foregoing pages have, perhaps, sufficiently demonstrated the nullity of the independence still acknowledged by the Ottoman Court to the constitution of its transdanubean Principalities, and the little regard it bears to the common prosperity of their affairs. That those countries should resume independency, and maintain themselves in it by their own means alone, would, however, be as absurd, as it is impossible to expect. But that they should be rescued from the hands of those who act as their worst enemies, and placed under the special protection of some great Christian power, under whose influence they might be enabled to employ their resources to their own profit and to that of their neighbours, give to their trade all the extent it is capable of compassing,—under which, in short they might have the hope of soon placing themselves on a footing with the civilised world—formed an object which called forth the attention of Christian Europe, and which, in magnitude and importance, had at least equal claims to it as the question relating to the Ionian Islands, to which the Turks had no smaller pretensions, though neither more nor less valid.

Conformity of religion, and the old standing connections between Russia and the principalities of Wallachia and Moldavia, point out that power as their natural protector; but, if the security of Europe forbids the recognition of further encroachments of the Russians on Turkey, though at the same time the political change in the principalities had been once regularly admitted, would not a partition made of them between Austria and Russia have been equally beneficial in its consequences, and at all events preferable in every respect to the *statu quo*? Indeed, upon the very principle of impeding the progress of Russia, the occupation of Wallachia by the Austrians was a measure of the first necessity, as sufficiently capable of forming an insurmountable barrier against the Russians. Without it, what obstacle will ever prevent these from extending the whole of their frontier on the side of European Turkey to the Danube? and once entirely masters of the borders of that river, the road to Constantinople is open to them, and the political existence of the Turkish empire is left to depend on the will and pleasure of the Russian emperor.

Austria, as long as she is willing to maintain her present extent of power, would certainly feel herself far from secure at the approach of the Russians on so great a line of her eastern frontiers, and would not tacitly consent to be severed from Turkey in a manner so as to alter materially the course of her communications with that country, and almost to preclude the possibility of affording it future assistance; neither would the rest of Europe, interested in obstructing the further designs of aggrandisement of Russia, view such an event without alarming apprehensions.

The precautions which the best political prudence could have suggested, ought, therefore, to have brought the Austrians into Wallachia, where they should have improved the fortifications at the most essential points. Such a measure, carried into execution, the Russians would in vain have attempted new encroachments; they could not have made one step into Turkey without the permission of the Austrians.

It has been said that the Russian plenipotentiaries at the congress of Vienna observed so profound a silence with respect to Turkish affairs, and so carefully avoided any opportunities of hearing them named, as to prove evidently, that in her concerns with that Power Russia wishes to remain her own arbiter. Perhaps, by that conduct, she prevented what she feared; for, had the partition of Wallachia and Moldavia been proposed to her, with the cession of the latter province to herself, could she possibly have brought forwards any reasonable objections? The arrangement would have appeared so suitable to all parties, that she could not have opposed it without betraying ambitious and subversive views; Turkey must have consented, if she bore any regard to her own future safety; and the inhabitants of the principalities, notwithstanding that they would in both have preferred the patronage of Russia to any interference of Austria, would soon have begun to feel the importance of the change in their favour.

What are the effects of the present system?—

The policy of the Turks in the principalities, renders them detestable to their inhabitants. They send men devoid of principles, bereft of all feelings of humanity, to exhibit a farce of sovereignty over them, and to display an arrogant and insulting power, in order to intimidate them into submission, and to impose with less difficulty an almost intolerable yoke. These agents of authority are looked upon by the two nations, whom they are sent to govern, not as their natural well-wishers, but as the chief enemies of the State; and the Turks being justly considered as the true authors of all their evils, the hand of vengeance is constantly raised over them, waiting for the opportunity when it can act with most efficacy.[44]

Russia is perfectly aware that such sentiments and dispositions constantly prevail amongst the Wallachians and Moldavians. The authority which she holds from her treaties with the Porte, enables her to interfere in all manner with their affairs, and to create, through their means, motives of discord between herself and Turkey whenever she finds a moment propitious to a rupture; and she may even, when she thinks proper, give an apparent urgency to such circumstances to justify any sudden seizure of the two provinces, operated without any previous declaration of war, and before the Porte could have entertained a suspicion of her intentions.

Turkey then, in being possessed of Wallachia and Moldavia on the present footing, is only favoured with a momentary advantage, very disproportionate to the danger of being involved through them in war against Russia, an event which must necessarily follow any attempts on the part of the latter to seize on the principalities, and which, according to the present political arrangements existing in Europe, would not fail to create again general convulsion.

From these considerations, it would appear evident, that as long as the transdanubean provinces continue to be a source of discord between Russia and Turkey, and as long as the important question relating to them remains unsettled, peace and tranquillity in Europe will only be of imaginary stability.

In the pacific sentiments which so eminently distinguish the Emperor Alexander, we have, indeed, a solid guarantee against any hostile attempts on Turkey; but the life of man being so precarious, is the hope of a long and uninterrupted peace to rest on the mere knowledge of that sovereign's personal character? And even if the Emperor Alexander should, contrary to present expectations, march his armies again into Moldavia and Wallachia, for the purpose of taking permanent possession of them, could we, in strict justice, accuse him of ambition in the performance of an act which common humanity dictates to any Christian power?

It is asserted that the success of the late great efforts against Buonaparte had, in a great measure, depended upon the Porte's forbearing to take a part against Russia, and that the allies, in order to induce the Turkish cabinet to adhere to the resolution it had evinced of remaining neutral, had promised to guarantee, whatever might happen, the integrity of the Ottoman empire; that the Porte, subsequently relying on this promise, declared itself entirely foreign to the objects in discussion at the congress of Vienna, and consequently was not invited to send ministers to it.

Now, that the co-operation of Turkey, with or against Russia and her allies, could have made the least impression on the destinies of Europe, at a time that the nation itself seemed so decidedly averse to the resumption of a war, and that the state was exhausted, appears most doubtful; but that the participation of the Turks in the transactions of the Congress might have settled affairs in a much more solid and lasting manner, is extremely probable. It is at that universal tribunal alone, formed for the vast purpose of creating a just and unchangeable equilibrium in the political affairs of Europe, that the Turks might have been made to understand and to feel the necessity of renouncing to possessions beyond the Danube, which, as they have no longer the means of maintaining and defending them, must, in their hands, continue to be a source of unceasing contentions, and a subject of wars, which will not only endanger the safety of the Ottoman empire, but also compromise the tranquillity of all Europe; and that the Danube being, in fact, the natural frontier of their present extent of empire in that part of it, is alone calculated to offer them security. And those tottering Ottomans, whose existence in Europe is already tolerated with too much indulgence, and who must be aware, notwithstanding the high opinion they entertain of their own importance, how much they are at the mercy of Christian powers, would they have ventured to combat any decisions of the congress which deprived them of a comparatively small extent of territory to enable them to preserve the remainder of their possessions in Europe? Could they have insisted upon the strict observance of former promises, when circumstances so important, concurring even to their own safety, revoked them, and whilst they themselves have, in many instances, been guilty of infractions to their very treaties?

No opportunity was ever, or will, perhaps, be again so favourable to the decision of this important question, as the Congress of Vienna; however, it passed there under general silence. This silence may indeed have originated in motives of great weight, but it could only have been of a momentary necessity, and probably it will not a little contribute to the causes of the first hostile shot that will be fired on the continent of Europe.

APPENDIX.

No. 1.
Translation of a Beratt, or Diploma, given by the present Sultan Mahmoud, Emperor Of Turkey, to Mr. Wilkinson.

The Emperor Sultan Mahmoud,

Son of Sultan Abdoulhammid

Ever Victorious!

By that glorious and imperial sign, I, who am the conqueror of the world, and whose authority is derived from Divine will,

Ordain as follows:

The Model of the Great amongst the nation of the Messiah, the Ambassador Extraordinary from the Court of Great Britain residing at my Sublime Porte, Robert Liston, (whose end be happiness,) has presented to my Imperial Porte an official note, by which he states that it is agreed by the Imperial capitulations that the English shall have the right to name consuls to Smyrna, Alexandria, Aleppo, Tripoli, Algiers, Tunis, and various other parts of my Empire; and that, when they wish to recall them no opposition shall be made: that in virtue of this agreement, Francis Summerers had been named the 3d of the Ramazan, 1217 (6th January 1802), consul-general in the principalities of Wallachia and Moldavia, (acknowledged by Imperial Beratt,) to protect the affair of the English merchants and other subjects who carry on business with those Countries, as well as to assist the passage of couriers and letters to and from England, and having resigned that office, the bearer of this Imperial document, one of the most noble of the nation of the Messiah, William Wilkinson, has been appointed consul-general in his place. The aforesaid Ambassador, in notifying his nomination, requests, that in virtue of the Imperial capitulations, this Imperial Beratt be given him.

Conforming myself to what has been hitherto practised and to the imperial capitulations, I give this imperial and august sign to the said William Wilkinson, and I ordain that he shall have henceforward the power of exercising the functions of British Consul in the aforesaid principalities; that he shall, according to the imperial capitulations, have to direct the public affairs of the English in Wallachia and Moldavia, and give every assistance with regard to the expedition of couriers and dispatches to and from England. All individuals, subjects of Great Britain, shall have to apply directly to him when they encounter difficulties in their affairs, and none must be permitted to depart from those Countries without being furnished with a passport from him.

It is not allowed that the servants of consuls be called upon to pay the capitation tax called *Haratsh*, nor the common contributions called *Avariz*, nor any of the arbitrary taxes and imposts levied under the name of *Russumus*, and *Tekaléfi-Urfié*. No one is permitted to demand of the consuls *Haratsh* or other contributions because they may have in their service slaves of the one or the other sex. No one shall molest them with regard to their private property, baggage, or provisions; and, according to former practice, they are exempted from custom-house and other duties for all such objects. And as consuls are the representatives of their governments, they shall never be arrested; their houses shall never be sealed, and no troops shall ever be quartered in them.

The abovementioned Consul, with his people and slaves, is therefore exempted from *Haratsh, Avariz, Hassabié-Ahtshessi*, and all other taxes, impositions, &c. If any one has a lawsuit with him, it shall be heard no where but at my Sublime Porte.

If the said Consul shall, at any time, wish to travel to any part of my dominions, he shall not be molested by any one, either going or coming, by sea or by land, in private houses or post-houses, neither for his baggage, equipages, or servants. Wherever he goes provisions shall be given him at the common prices of the market, and no one shall have to make the least difficulty. Wherever he may meet with danger he is at liberty to wear the Turkish dress with the white turban, as also any military dress with the sabre, bow and arrows, spurs, &c. The princes, governors, and other officers, not only shall not molest him, but shall likewise give him every assistance and attention.

All such as do not abide by these orders shall be punished accordingly. Every one is to conform himself to the Imperial capitulations, and to my glorious signature which prescribes submission; no contrary proceeding shall be permitted or tolerated.

Given at my Imperial residence of Constantinople the well-guarded, 24th Gemassielevel, 1229. (24th May, 1814.)

APPENDIX, No. 2.
Additional Articles to the Treaty signed at Kaïnargik, the 10th July, 1775, relating to Wallachia, Moldavia, &c.

The Court of Russia restores to the Sublime Porte the whole province of Bessarabba, with its fortified places, viz. Akkerman, Killia, Ismaïl, Bender, and the other towns and villages within that province; as well as the principalities of Wallachia and Moldavia, with the fortresses, capitals, towns, and villages belonging to them.

The Sublime Porte, in taking possession of them, solemnly engages to observe the following conditions, without the least deviation:—

1st. To acknowledge and maintain the constitutions of the two principalities, the established customs, rank, dignities, property, and churches of the two nations, without any exception whatever: to give them total amnesty and pardon conformably to the 1st article of the general treaty: to leave unmolested all such persons as have not remained faithful to the Ottoman interest; to admit them to their former ranks, and to restore to them any property and possessions they had previous to the war.

2d. To oppose no sort of difficulty to the free exercise of the Christian religion in the said principalities, nor to the repair or construction of churches and other buildings.

3d. To restore to the monasteries in the neighbourhood of Ibraïl, Hotim, and Bender, all the property belonging to them, and which had, contrary to justice, been taken from them.

4th. To acknowledge and bear all due regard to the ecclesiastical order.

5th. To permit those families and individuals who have any desire of retiring to Russia, or elsewhere, to depart freely with their moveable property, and to allow them a year's time previous to such departure that they may settle their affairs in the country.

6th. To renounce entirely the payment of old accounts, for whatever relates to former contributions.

7th. To claim no tribute from the inhabitants of the said province and principalities for the space of time that they have been occupied by the Russians, and in consideration of the losses and sufferings sustained by them on account of the war, to claim no sort of tribute from them for the space of two years after the date of the treaty.

8th. The Porte engages to show every regard and humanity to the inhabitants of the said countries, at and after the expiration of the term mentioned in the 7th article, relative to the tribute and taxes which they shall then be called upon to pay, and will neither suffer nor permit any Pasha or other person, to oppress and molest them after the payment of the ordinary tribute. And also to allow them the free and entire exercise of the privileges they enjoyed during the reign of Sultan Mehmet 4th, father to the present Sultan. And the Porte shall permit the Hospodars of Wallachia and Moldavia to have one or more public agents to reside at Constantinople, Greeks by nation or religion, who shall have to transact the affairs of the princes; and not only consents to acknowledge and treat with them, but also promises to observe in them the privileges due to persons who treat public rights and interests, and are not under the controul of power.

The Sublime Porte also acknowledges and admits, that the Russian ministers residing at Constantinople, shall have the right of interfering in behalf of the affairs of the two principalities abovementioned, and engages to pay every regard to their representations.[45]

APPENDIX, No. 3.
Extracts of Two Letters written from Bukorest to Mr. Wilkinson, in London, containing the particulars of Prince Caradga's fight from Wallachia.

On the 7th instant (October, 1818), a messenger arrived in three days from Constantinople to the Prince, and in the course of the same day, a report was circulated all over the town, that the prince was preparing to depart. On the following morning the Postelnik Vlaccuzzi, with his wife[46] and family, was seen to go out of town in a travelling carriage, and great preparations of departure being continued at court, the rumours increased, and people began to be alarmed.

On Sunday the 11th, after the accustomed ceremonial at court of the Turkish Baïram, the prince conferred titles on several persons, and made changes in the public offices. In the afternoon he accompanied the funeral procession of the old Bann Golesko, and on his return home, he called the Spathar Balliano, the Aga Vakaresko, and a few others into his closet, and informed them that his life being in danger if he continued longer in the country, he was on the point of departure. He recommended a good police regulation to maintain order and tranquillity, and he named a provisional government composed of the metropolitan, Brancovano, and Samourkash, whom he instructed to act during his absence, until the Porte should determine on new measures of administration. He also sent for the Russian Consul-General Mr. Pini, and after having prevailed on him to take charge of such private concerns as he had not had time to settle, he took a friendly leave of them all, and got into his ordinary *calèche*, attended by two servants only, as if going to take his usual evening drive. He repaired to Banessa, where he was joined by the princess his wife, the princess Rallou his daughter, and her husband the Bann Argiropulo, the young prince Constantine, the Postelnik Mavrocordato, the Aga Vlangalli, and a few servants, who were all waiting with travelling carriages and post-horses, baggage, &c. They all set out together, and at a mile's distance from Banessa, they were joined by four hundred Albanians, (the prince's body-guards) well mounted and well armed. They directed their course to Kronstadt in Transylvania, where they arrived in safety, after four days journey, and were well received by the Austrian General commanding on the frontiers.

The four hundred guards were sent back, and the Prince, whilst on the road, transmitted various orders to the provisional government, as if he continued to be the only chief of the country.

It is said he will not stop long at Kronstadt, but will proceed on to Switzerland, where he intends to fix his abode.

Immediately after his departure, the Russian consul placed the imperial seal on all the apartments of the court, some of which contained furniture, and other articles of much value, after which he laid a formal sequester upon the Prince's private property, under the plea that he had left unpaid several debts to Russian merchants.

All the Boyars assembled on the 12th, and wrote to the Porte the particulars of this unexpected event, they have since held several deliberations, and have finally agreed to send a petition to the Sultan, representing all the miseries to which they were exposed under the administration of Greek Princes, praying that he would henceforward confide the government of the principality to the Divan alone, and engaging themselves to observe faithfully all the conditions that have been hitherto prescribed to the Hospodars. We are now waiting with anxiety to learn the nature of the measures that the Porte will deem most proper to adopt, and the moment is of no small importance to the fate of this country. Meanwhile we live under continual apprehension that the Turkish Pashahs of the neighbourhood may take upon themselves to send troops in order to occupy the country, a circumstance which, instead of producing the good effects of precaution, will throw every thing into confusion and disorder, and frighten away a great number of families, who, in that expectation, are already making preparations to retire into Transylvania and Moldavia.

10th December.—Every thing went on quietly. The Sultan, after deliberating in his council on the subject of the Boyars' petition, has refused to comply with their demand, and has appointed Prince Alexander Sutzo new Hospodar of Wallachia. His Caïmacams have already arrived, and have taken the momentary direction of public affairs. We know for certain that Prince Caradja, who has left Kronstadt, will fix his residence at Geneva.

APPENDIX, No. 4.
Derivation of various words in the Wallachian or Moldavian language, from the Latin, Italian, Greek, and Turkish.

Wallachian.	Latin.	English.
Domno	Dominus	Lord.
Formos	Formosus	Handsome.
Massa	Mensa	Table.
Cappo	Caput	Head.
Venat	Venatio	Game.
Vorba	Verbum	Word.
Alb	Albus	White.
Sunt	Sunt	I am.
Lacrymæ	Lacrymæ	Tears.
Bunn	Bonus	Good.
Respuns	Responsum	Answer.
Pallatur	Palatium	Palace.
Pescator	Piscator	Fisher.
Pritshep	Percipio	I understand.
Luminar	Lume	Light.
Locul	Locus	Place.
Dzio	Dies	Day.
Degete	Digiti	Fingers.
Negro	Negrum	Black.
Nushtio	Nescio	I know not.
Scamn	Scamnum	Chair.
Vitric	Vitricus	Glass.
Incep	Incipio	I begin.
Ris	Ris	To laugh.
Böo	Bos	An Ox.

Parinte	Parens	Parents.
Unde	Unde	Where.
Cum	Cum	With.

Wallachian.	**Italian.**	**English.**
Luna	Luna	Moon.
Firestra	Finestra	Window.
Fier	Ferro	Iron.
Porta	Porta	Door.
Ochi	Ochi	Eyes.
Limba	Lingua	Tongue.
Puine	Pane	Bread.
Appa	Aqua	Water.
Mancare	Manggiare	To eat.
Nopte	Notti	Night.
Muna	Mano	Hand.
Frunte	Fronte	Forehead.
Dintz	Denti	Teeth.
Camascia	Camicia	Shirt.
Bine	Bene	Well.
Ann	Anno	Year.
Acro	Acro	Sour.
Argint	Argento	Silver.
Aür	Oro	Gold.
Peshte	Pesce	Fish.
Naz	Naso	Nose.
Occit	Accetto	Vinegar.
Pace	Pace	Peace.

Amavut	Ho avuto	I have had.
Ce fatshe	Che fate?	What are you doing?
Dorm	Dormo	I sleep.
Battut	Battuto	Beaten.
Cal	Cavallo	Horse.
Clappon	Cappone	Capon.
Tsara	Terra	Land.
Dattor	Debitore	Debtor.
Dinderet	Di dietro	Backwards.
Drept	Dritto	Right.
Dreptate	Rectitudine	Rectitude.
Disfacut	Disfatto	Undone.
Morte	Morte	Death.
Greo	Grave	Grave.
Genuchi	Ginschia	Knees.
Cuïna	Cucina	Kitchen.
Fericit	Felice	Happy.
Nefericit	Infelice	Unhappy.
Cumper	Comprare	To purchase,
Unire	Unire	To unite.
Vin	Vino	Wine.
Vie	Vigna	Vineyard.
Mio	Mio	Mine.
Cassa	Casa	House.
Miere	Mielle	Honey.
Place	Piace	To please.
Remast	Rimasto	To remain.

Pling	Piango	To weep.
Gustare	Gustare	To taste.
Viatsa	Vita	Life.
Striga	Strilla	To scream.
Stregoica	Strega	A witch.
Inghietsit	Inghiottito	To swallow.
Agiun	Digiuno	Fasting.
Dulce	Dolce	Sweet.
Amar	Amaro	Bitter.
Musica	Musica	Music.
Fuoc	Fuocco	Fire.
Dulceazza	Dolcezza	Sweet-meats.
Kimpo-lung	Campo-lango	Long-field.
Wallachian Numerals:—uno, doï, tre, patro, cintsh, shasse, shapte, aht, noo, zece.		
Italian Numerals:—uno, due, tre, quattro, cinque, sei, sette, otto, nove, dieu.		
Ce hai scris?	Cosa hai scritto?	What have you written?
N'hai faccutto bine.	Non hai fatto bene.	It is not well done.
Adam parinte al nostro ha peccattuit.	Adam padrie nostro ha peccatto.	Our father Adam has sinned.
Christos ha patsit pentro peccattele nostre.	Christo ha patito per li peccati nostri.	Christ has suffered for our sins.
Voi se intra la shola.	Voglio intrar 'nella schola.	I wish to enter the school.
Ha perdutt viatza.	Ha perduto la vita.	He has lost his life.

Wallachian.	Modern Greek.	English.
Pajoss	πεζός	Pedestrian.
Sindrofia	σινδροφία	Company.
Daskal	δάσκαλος	Tutor, or rather School-master.
Affanissit	αφανισμένος	Ruined.
Ha costissit	εκόστισεν	The cost in a purchase.
Peristassis	περίστασις	Circumstance.
Ifos	ύφος	Arrogance.
Procopsit	προκομένος	a clever man.
Pnevma	πνεύμα	Wit.
Katandissit	κατανδισμένος	reduced in circumstances.
Droom	δρόμος	Road.
M'am aposessit	απόρεσα	I was astonished.
Zahar	ζάχαρι	Sugar.
Pethepsit	πεδευμένος	Punished.
Kindin	κίνδινο	Risk or danger.
Periorissit	περιορισμένος	Engaged.
Thiazeeon	διαζίων	Act of divorce.
Yeftin	φθινό	Cheap.
Tropos	τρόπος	Means.
Mere	μίλα	Apples.
Ipokeemen	υποχίνενος	An individual.
Thiathisis	διάθισις	a strong desire.
Proerisis	προέρισις	Inclination.
Simandicos	σιμανδιχός	a person of note.
Staré	στάσιμον	State, or situation.
Kivernisis	χιβέρνισις	a living.

Wallachian.	Turkish.	English.
Perdé	Perdé	Curtain
Duckian	Duckian	Shop
Chismé	Chismé	Boots.
Paputsh	Paputsh	Shoes.
Chiorap	Chiorap	Stockings.
Shapka	Shapka	Hat.
Ocka	Ocka	an Oke (weight).
Dram	Dram	a Dram.
Massalla	Mashalla	a Flambeau.

APPENDIX, No. 5.

An explanation of the Nizam-y-Gedid institution, and some curious remarks concerning it. Written by Tshelebi-Effendi, one of the chief dignitaries of the Ottoman Empire, Counsellor, Minister of State, &c. and translated from the original Turkish manuscript.

PREFACE.

The most high God, who hath willed that the race of the children of Adam should endure from the time of Adam, even unto the day of judgment, hath, by the mysterious decrees of his Divine Providence, created an Emperor of the world, to administer with justice the affairs of the whole company of his servants, and to protect them from their enemies.[47]

It is by repelling hostile violence that the affairs of the world are maintained in due order; since the Divine Majesty hath subjected the earth to government in such a manner that it is divided into many regions, each of them should have its own Sovereign, and that the places subject to each Sovereign, and the servants of God whom they contain, should find in their rulers (each according to the power he possesses, and the age in which he lives) a protection and security from the malice and treachery of their hostile neighbours and other enemies.

As those States which guard against dishonour, and by daily improving and confirming their system of government, obtain in these respects a superiority over the neighbouring nations, have flourished accordingly; in like manner, decay and destruction have been the lot of such as in these points have been inferior to the countries adjoining them; because it is the invariable nature of the children of Adam to lengthen the hand against the dominion and wealth of the weak and indolent.

It is said in the history which treats of the terms of peace concluded by the sublime person who has received the mercy of God[48], that those States which from carelessness did not take proper precautions to guard against the violence of strangers, have remained without either honour or reputation, and dependent upon others. Or even from the consequence of their negligence, having fallen entirely into the hands of foreigners, their kings have become subjects, and their rich men poor. It is a principle to be observed by those who rule governments, and are men of understanding and penetration, that, "even if your enemy is an ant, you should use every effort against him;" that conformably to this proverb, they may not suffer themselves to be brought into calamity, by the treacherous machinations of the neighbouring States, and other hostile nations.

The purpose of this preface is as follows:—In the period which elapsed from the year 1150 to the year 1182 of the Hejira, the greatest part of those who had seen service before the conclusion of the wars, went to the confines of nonexistence.[49] And those who had not seen service, having never travelled an hour's journey from home, were entirely ignorant of the affairs of the enemies of religion.[50] It followed that the greater part of the inhabitants of the Sublime Empire[51] lived in an easy, careless manner, and had never experienced the vicissitudes of fortune. The corruption and disorder that prevailed in the discipline of our troops during the Russian war which broke out in the year 1182[52], gave rise to the confusion in which the world has been involved from that time to this, a space of near forty years. Although the truth of this is evident to a few men of sagacity and penetration, who, remaining from the former generation, may be enumerated out of the vulgar herd, yet, on account of the situation in which the world is, and the circumstances of the times, most of them are obliged, in their discourse, to appear to agree with the opinions of the people at large.

For some time past, a rabble composed of the dregs of the populace, setting themselves up for judges of the times, and assembling in the coffee-houses, barbers' shops, and taverns, have, in vain speeches, unbecoming their station, indulged themselves in the liberty of abusing and calumniating the Sublime Government; and as they have not been visited by the punishment which they deserve, people of this sort have thence been emboldened to say whatever they please. This system has often brought the Sublime Government into trouble.

In the times of Suleÿman Khan Kannuni[53] the Just, a few ignorant men who did not approve of the new system then promulgated, having got together in one place, railed against the Sublime Government, uttering whatever tedious and absurd speeches came uppermost in their mouths. This circumstance coming to the knowledge of the Emperor, he cut off the ears and tongues both of the railers and listeners, and nailed them, for an example to the world, on the upper porch of a small gate near the palace of Sultan Bayazid. As this place was a thoroughfare for the public, all those who with their eyes contemplated the sight, learned to restrain their tongues. At that time, as at the present period, the greater part of the vulgar, in their ingratitude for benefits conferred, resembled the children of Ismael. This sort of rabble being ignorant that from themselves springs the corruption of the world, give their opinions on affairs as though they had by inspiration received intuitive knowledge of them, and taking no blame to themselves, as though their own inertness was not the cause of such misfortunes, have rendered themselves the devil's laughing stock. As no public examples are made of them, owing to the lenity which now prevails, and to certain considerations, the temper of these times is neither fit for peace or war, and is incapable of rendering service to government and religion. Nevertheless, that the world may not remain empty, a company of hogs, corrupt and degraded like those who preceded them, assemble in taverns, coffee-houses, and brothels, in order to abuse and vilify the Sublime Government. This perverse race are outwardly Mussulmans[54], yet have they not the least idea of religious purity, and are indeed a collection of baccals[55], boatmen, fishermen, porters, coffee-house keepers, and such like persons.[56] Although it would be requisite to punish many of them for opening their mouths on state matters, and to make public examples of them for the purpose of restoring order to the world, yet the force of necessity obliges the government to overlook their faults.

A treatise which should contain an accurate account of the consequences produced by the insolence and folly of the vulgar of this day, and especially a correct statement of some events which ought to be made public, having been required of us from the highest quarter, we have undertaken to write it in a style which is simple, and easy to be understood. Under the Divine favor, those who study this book with sentiments of religion, will thereby be enabled to make themselves acquainted with the present condition of the world.

SECTION I.
An Explanation of the Causes which have occasioned Trouble in the World.

"This institution of the Nizam-y-Gedid has caused the established order of the world to be disturbed, and has given cause to the insolent conduct of the mountaineers in the country of Rumelia." Such are the expressions employed by a set of contentious and ignorant men, incapable of learning reason. I have sometimes questioned such persons, saying as follows:—"Ho, friend! allow me in the first place to ask you a question. What is this institution against which you make such continual and senseless outcry? First know precisely what it is, and then continue to oppose it. If there be reason in what you say, I am open to conviction, and am ready to concede the point in dispute." On hearing this, all they could say was, that what they call the Nizam-y-Gedid, is a body of troops trained and exercised; beyond which, and a mere profession of their aversion to it, they plainly showed that they knew nothing about the matter. Although I saw that an attempt to make this kind of rabble understand public affairs, is like trying to make a camel leap over a ditch, I proceeded to put some questions that occurred to me, as follows:—"Shall I give you some account of the troubles which occurred in the world before the Nizam-y-Gedid existed, during the reigns of their highnesses the former Ottoman Sultans, who have found mercy from God? Such as the disturbances raised in Anatolia by the Gellalli[57], and the insolence of Sarry Beÿ Oglou in the reign of Sultan Mahmoud, and especially the events which passed in Egypt, occasioned by Sacka-Yorghi Alli-Beÿ, the son of a glass-blower; and the affairs of Emir-Daher, of Abou-Vahib, all of which happened during the reign of Sultan Moustapha; and the calamities inflicted by the unemployed Levendis,[58] who turned the province of Anatolia upside down; and the continued bad success which attended the arms of the followers of Islam, for the space of seven years, during the Muscovite war, which began in the year 1182; the defeats which our great armies suffered every year, with the loss of so many thousand tents, such abundance of camp equipage, treasure, artillery, bombs, and military stores, sufficient for the consumption of many years, and so great a loss of our troops, either taken, drowned, or killed, and the capture as well of our small forts and retrenched posts, as of our large fortresses, some of which were reduced by famine and others by force; and the impossibility of delivering so many thousand women and children whom they contained, and who, still remaining in captivity, pass their lives in tears. These are things, the bitter remembrance of which can never be erased from our hearts. Some of these calamitous events may be found in our annals, and some have happened in our days. Pray was the Nizam-y-Gedid the cause of all these disorders and disgraceful occurrences? It did not exist at that time, and yet you see that confusion was already introduced, and the regular order of things interrupted. Is then the Nizam-y-Gedid the only cause of revolution? On what does your dispute now rest, and what answer can you give to my question?" After I had thus spoken, some of them who were disposed to hear reason yielded to conviction, and remained abashed, having nothing to answer. But some others, less reasonable, who knew nothing of the things which I had spoken, answered thus:—"What need I know about the troubles that have formerly happened in the world? I am well aware that those which now prevail are caused by the Nizam-y-Gedid." To these ignorant and pertinacious adversaries, I again addressed myself in these terms:—"Disturbances having broken out in the regions of France, the people eat each other's flesh[59], and the Crals[60] having declared war against them, for the space of exactly fifteen years, battles have been fought without intermission, so that the country of France has been turned upside down, and the inhabitants have drank each other's blood, and poured it out in the streets like a torrent, and have, until this day, with the fury of dogs, changed their country into a slaughter-house for swine. Behold such troubles are not confined to[61] Frenghistan alone. Neither India, nor China, Arabia, Persia, nor the new world[62], are at present exempt from confusion and carnage. These things being so, is their source to be attributed to the Nizam-y-Gedid? We may observe, likewise, that although trouble and bloodshed prevail in Rumelia, yet, thanks be to God, Anatolia is free from these calamities (may the ears of Satan be stopped with lead[63]). Shall we say, then, that the fatal contagion of the Nizam-y-Gedid is confined to Rumelia, and that it has not infected Anatolia; or rather have not these things proceeded from the decrees of Providence? Should not that consideration strike us? After reflecting and meditating on what I have said, what reply can you make?"—"Good God!" says my opponent, "I thought Rumelia alone had been disturbed."—"Then," I replied, "if you are ignorant that every part of the world is thus convulsed, and such things happen when there is no Nizam-y-Gedid, and disturb the tranquillity of the universe, you should not, by any means, impute the origin of dissension to that establishment."

By thus addressing them, I succeeded, by Divine favour, in bringing many of them to conviction. With respect to those persons, who, although they are acquainted with the true origin of such events, and the course of worldly affairs, and understand and know the commands of the great Prophet (on whom be salvation and the peace of God), yet persevere in their perverse opposition; and who, because they were formerly authors of sedition, are ashamed to belie their words, and therefore maintain the dispute, and uphold contention; who, having originally calumniated the corps of cannoneers of the Nizam-y-Gedid, and abuse those who were the authors of it, uttering speeches which do not become their lips, on a subject above their comprehension; with respect, I say, to such persons, who, although they themselves confessed that the excellence of these new troops was seen in the French war, and that to their good conduct many of us owed our escape from captivity, yet afterwards forgetting this avowal, are not ashamed to indulge in extravagant abuse of them, it remains only, that at the five stated times of prayer, we beseech the Divine Providence to grant them understanding, and a knowledge of the right way, that they may distinguish good from evil, and acknowledge the power of the Sublime Government with whose bread they are fed; and that thus, by a sincere union of hearts in the way of truth and justice, we may obtain complete success over the enemies of the state and of our religion. Thus did I manage my dispute and conference with those adversaries who attributed to the Nizam-y-Gedid the troubles of the world. Long and tedious indeed it was; yet by the favour of the Divine Majesty, and the protection of the great Prophet of miraculous memory, many of the opponents, who were at first unwilling to hear reason, have been convinced, and brought to entertain a just idea of those affairs; and using their efforts to convince others, have entered into the congregation of well-wishers to government.

SECTION II.
An Explanation of the Causes which gave rise to the Establishment of this Nizam-y-Gedid, about which so much noise has been made.

Be it known to men of understanding, that after the conclusion of peace with the Muscovite infidels, in the year 1206[64], when ambassadors were passing to and fro, at the time that the prisoners were released, diligent enquiry was made of many persons who had been in the hands of the Russians, with regard to the power and condition of the enemies of our faith. In the city called Petersburgh, which is the residence of the Russian sovereign, are to be found men of all nations. Among these was a certain infidel, formerly an

Ottoman Rayah, but fixed, by his employments, in the Russian states; a man extremely rich, and a complete master of the art of deceit, acute and lively in speech, and devoid of shame and modesty.

This man, who was at that time become an ambassador[65] said one day to the[66]sovereign, in a familiar society of Franks[67], "Why should you give yourself the trouble of carrying on long and obstinate wars with the Ottomans? If your design be to take Constantinople, why should you, by carrying on operations on the land side, struggle with so many difficulties? Nothing is more easy than the capture of Constantinople." On the sovereign's desiring to know which was this easy method, the wicked person answered as follows:—"The *Cralyä*[68] having formerly carried on two or three successful wars, and possessed herself of the kingdom of the Crimea, equipped a fleet on the Black Sea, and after annihilating the Tartar nation, and taking many forts and castles, reduced to her obedience the rayahs of the White Sea[69] and many trading communities, it would be easy, by following up a certain plan, to accomplish in two days the conquest of Constantinople, which need only be attacked by a single streight." The Cralyä, pleased with this suggestion, said, "If you prove yourself useful in rendering me that service, I will appoint you King of Constantinople for the term of your life, in the same way that I appointed a king over the country of Poland." The person then spoke again thus:—"None of all the Ottoman troops are now ready to take the field: those of Anatolia are employed in cultivating the land, and smoking their pipes; such as inhabit Constantinople are either busied in carrying on various trades, or at least are not subject to any good discipline. Were they to assemble troops with the greatest possible expedition, they would require at least a month for that purpose. Behold, the water used for drinking in so great a city, comes from certain reservoirs which are without it.[70] It is not, therefore, expedient for us to carry on a troublesome war with ships and troops by sea and by land. We need only dispatch to the Crimea all the Russian ships that are in the White Sea, and there, filling with troops all our vessels, large and small, we will disembark them suddenly without the channel of the Black Sea, in the district that contains the reservoirs, the walls of which we will beat down with our cannon and[71]destroy. In one hour this may be effected. On the waters running out, the consequence will be a great tumult at Constantinople, the news being every where spread that the Russians have destroyed the reservoirs of water, that they are about to assault Constantinople with all their forces, and that their ulterior projects are not known. In the space of one day the want of water will produce confusion among them, which will be augmented by our zealous partisans of the Greek nation. The troops which are in Constantinople, instead of marching immediately against us, will pillage the public treasures, and those of their emperor, ministers, and rich men; and putting their booty hastily on board such boats and vessels as they find at hand, will endeavour to fly to Anatolia and elsewhere. The residue of the inhabitants, who remain at Constantinople, being left to themselves in this calamity, and overwhelmed with astonishment, having no water to bake bread, or to drink, will, in the course of two days, be reduced to the last extremity. So that the Russian troops, gradually advancing and entering the city, will make themselves entire masters of it."

The Sublime Government having received intelligence of this conversation, and of the decision taken in consequence of it[72], the infernal treachery of the aforesaid wicked person, seemed really to have conceived a feasible project. Water sleeps, and enemy is sleepless.[73] It is especially to be considered, that the distance from the peninsula of the Crimea to the channel of the Black Sea, is such, that a ship may cross it without altering a sail; and whatever confidence we may place in our own strength, yet, God forbid that so cunning an enemy should find us in an unguarded posture; particularly since we are instructed by the example of so many States, that owed their loss of reputation and ruin to the want of care in observing the machinations of their enemies, and in neglecting to provide in proper time efficient troops and military stores. From this source their calamities have arisen, as is written and set forth, as well in other histories, as in that which treats of the misfortune of the Sublime Person, who has received the mercy of[74]God, and of the peace which he concluded. The Russian infidels having withal greatly improved the state of their dominions within the space of seventy or eighty years, and manifested their thirst of glory by their arrogant and insolent interference in the interior affairs of other States, and having annexed several foreign countries to their own dominions, especially the kingdom of Poland, we must not, by any means, consider ourselves secure from so treacherous and deceitful a nation. Besides all this, the upright and provident ministers of the Sublime Government, who are aware of the evil designs of the enemy, having represented to the Emperor, (who is at the summit of power, and inhabits the mansions of wisdom and understanding,) that if such an attempt as that suggested to the Cralyä by the before-mentioned reprobate, should actually take place against the reservoirs, (which God forbid!) as there had been no care taken to provide either money or troops, it would be utterly impossible to dispatch with expedition against the enemy forces that were under no discipline, or to repulse them with such soldiers; and that the people of the Empire of Islam, reposing entirely on the protection of Providence, would not make the least resistance. That therefore, as it was a maxim established that in an urgent case, when some remedy must be sought, resources must be found in the whole body of those who are attached to government, without consulting the lower orders; there was no other method of dispelling and removing the danger we have spoken of above, but by keeping a body of troops on foot ready for service. It was also taken into consideration, that even if the description of force required for the purpose really existed at Constantinople; yet in case of any danger arising on the side of the reservoirs in the way we have mentioned, (which Heaven forbid!) as the intelligence must be conveyed from thence to Constantinople, and as the troops must assemble, it would require five days at least before they could reach their destination. May God protect and guard us! "The serpent kills a man in Egypt whilst the Teryak[75] is coming from Venice," as the proverb says.

With regard to the apprehensions entertained for the reservoirs, it appeared in every case indispensably necessary, that on that side a body of troops should be kept in readiness in some fixed station, and provided with requisite supply of artillery, ammunition, and military stores; and such troops as should not, like the rest of our forces, be composed of sellers of pastry, boatmen, fishermen, coffee-house keepers, baccals, and others who are engaged in the thirty-two trades, but of well disciplined men, who would take care to have their cannon and muskets ready for service, and on an urgent occasion, would be prepared in the space of half an hour to engage the troops and artillery of the enemy; to repulse them, and retaliate on them their own hostile devices. After these points had been taken into serious consideration, some men were in the first place dispatched to the corps of the Janissaries for the purpose of selecting from thence some young and chosen soldiers, whom they were to discipline and train to the use of arms. Upon this, our bravoes who are engaged in the thirty-two trades, considering that if they were obliged to attend punctually to the exercise of cannon and small arms, they would be occupied with that instead of their private affairs, and would be brought into trouble, no longer receiving their pay once in three months gratuitously, and without doing any thing for it, began to ponder the matter, stroaking their beards and mustachios, and to vent their discontent by saying, "We are not made for this sort of work, and we will have nothing to do with it." Whatever pains were taken to enlighten their understandings, they obstinately persisted, addressing each other by these or similar terms, "Ho! Alli Sacka Baba, Oda Bashi, Bash Karakouloukgee![76] what say you to this business? the exercise of the Nizam-y-Gedid is now introduced; henceforth no pay is to be had without service, and what they call exercise is a very troublesome service; it is true that drawing up in a line makes a better show; but if they send us to war, we can fire our muskets, and then charging sword in hand, we can put the Russians to flight and storm their camp. May Heaven preserve from decay our corps and our chiefs! we shall then take our pay when it is issued, and pass our time agreeably." Such were their expressions, as though they could by frigid reasoning, and senseless allusions, induce the Sublime Government to abandon this enterprise, when the experience of two wars had proved, beyond dispute, both the total inefficiency of their services, and the feeble condition of the Mahometan community.

With respect to the apprehensions entertained of the destruction of those fine reservoirs by the Russian infidels, the first step which was taken for the purpose of procuring speedy and effectual means of guarding against so devilish a piece of treachery, consisted in an ordinance for levying a body of Bostangees[77], who were to be quartered at the Levend-Chifflick, a military post newly established at no great distance from the reservoirs, in order that in an urgent crisis when we fly for refuge to Divine protection, they might be ready for service in a very short space of time. But the most important point is this: that the new levied troops, instead of engaging in trade, should remain day and night in their quarters, applying themselves daily to military exercises, and keeping their arms, cannon, muskets, and warlike implements of every description necessary for immediate service; thus practising a discipline suitable to their appellation of soldiers of the new regulation. To complete all, every Orta[78] led an *Imam*[79] attached to it for the due performance of religious worship, that nothing requisite might be omitted. Besides this, numerous batteries are established on the shores of the canal of the Black Sea[80], well furnished with artillery, and a sufficient number of gunners were appointed to serve them, and to oppose any attempt which might be made by the enemies of our faith, to force the passage of the said canal. As the perfect discipline of the garrisons of those forts, rendered the passage of a ship altogether impracticable, the enemies of our faith clearly saw that the attempt must end in their destruction; and thus, under the Divine favour, their wicked projects, which we have already related, were rendered fruitless and abortive.

The continual and daily progress which these new soldiers have been making in discipline and order, and the excellent conduct and steady valour which a handful of our regular troops displayed at Alexandria, Cairo, and Acre, have caused the hearts of the foes of our religion to melt within them, on seeing and hearing these things. We trust, that by the favour of Heaven, when this description of our force called Nizam-y-Gedid shall have become sufficiently numerous, terror and consternation will take possession of the hearts of the Russians, the Germans, and the other enemies of our faith and Empire, to such a degree, that they will no longer think of imposing on the Sublime Government hard and insolent conditions; and that, lastly, this institution of regular soldiers, proceeding from the habitation of the great Spirit which rules over our faith and Empire, will perpetuate the duration of the Sublime Government even to the end of the world, and will give us victory over all our enemies.

It has happened to me a thousand times to find myself engaged in dispute with a crowd of contentious fools, who say, "Is there any occasion for these new troops of the Nyzam-y-Gedid? At the time that the Ottoman race conquered the world with the sabre, there were no such forces. Let the enemy present himself, and we will lay our hands on our sabres, and at a single charge make piece-meal of them. Only let us see the intentions of our enemy, we will storm their camp, sword in hand, upset their Cral from his throne, trample his crown under our feet, and penetrate even to the most distant of their countries."

To these bravoes I thus addressed myself: "Hark ye, comrade! do you know that ever since the year 1146 I, as well as my father, have served with all my might in the corps of Janissaries, and have been engaged in several wars, and have seen the world both hot and cold, and feeding from the world's basket, have passed through the hoop of the elements.[81] Having moreover been a prisoner in the hands of the enemies of religion, I became fully acquainted with their deceit and treachery, their discipline, and the successes which they have obtained over the Sublime Government. It has thus been easy for me to gain an intimate knowledge of many things, the truth of which cannot be easily understood from the mere perusal of our annals. As I am now eighty-seven years of age, if all those affairs that have passed since the year 82, with which I am thoroughly conversant, were to be written, they would fill several volumes. There are, however, certain events taken as well from history as from what has fallen under my own observation, which I wish to relate to you; and as my discourse shall be free from malevolence and bad passions, I trust in God that you will hear me with satisfaction, and will one day bless me."

SECTION III.

The subject that we are now to treat is as follows:—

At the accession to the throne of that flower of Emperors, Sultan Suleÿman Kannuni, the science of firing with quickness artillery in position, making use of muskets, and practising such like military exercises, and of defeating large armies with a very small body of troops, was not known amongst the foreign states of Europe and other nations. In this state of things they carried on wars against us; and in such contests the pious enthusiasm of the soldiers of Islam caused the gales of victory and conquest to blow on the side of the Sublime Government. Sometimes, also, they were on that of the enemy. It came to pass by a disposition of Divine Providence, that His Highness Sultan Suleÿman having for some years following continually met with bad success in his wars against the Germans, and perceiving that his defeats were owing to the unskilfulness and want of discipline of our soldiers, employed himself in creating a corps of regular troops[82], and inscribing recruits for that purpose. Immediately a number of idle and ignorant vagabonds, who disapproved of this institution of troops, quarters, and military regulations, began to murmur, saying, "Was the world originally conquered by the

Janissaries? No; it was subdued by the Segbans, and other valiant companies.[83] What sort of corps is this? and what is the meaning of these dresses? What strange things are the water-carriers, cooks, and servants, with their various dresses and titles!" By disseminating these seditious speeches, they entirely corrupted the minds of those soldiers who had been, or were to be enrolled in the new corps of Janissaries. So that, for instance, if an hundred recruits had their names inscribed to-day, to-morrow two hundred would desert.

His Highness the said Emperor, reflecting on what passed, and considering the favour which had been granted by Divine Providence to our magnificent Lord[84]; understanding also that every age was gifted with some polar star of intellectual excellence, discovered that there existed at that period from among the sons and successors of Hagee Bektash, the polar star of the times. The Emperor having caused this personage to be brought to him from Anatolia, spoke to him of the new corps which he had formed for the purpose of snatching victory from the infidels, and giving it to the people of Islam, and demanded the prayers of this Sheich, that the soldiers enrolled in the corps, instead of deserting, might display constancy and firmness. The said personage having therefore prayed, from that day forth the recruits no longer fled, but looking upon themselves as the children of Hagee-Bektash, firmly persevered in their service; and thus, when expeditions were undertaken against the enemy by these regular troops, who were kept closely to the pitch of discipline necessary at that time, the happy influence as well of the Emperor of Islam who is the chief of religious conquerors, as of the aforesaid holy personage, had so beneficial an effect, that they overthrew the armies of the enemies of the faith, and gained such signal advantages, that were we to describe them at large, our discourse would be too prolix. Before much time had elapsed, the enemy being broken and routed, and perceiving by experience the advantages of this discipline, obtained peace with a thousand entreaties. Hereupon all the Crals[85] being seized with consternation, after communicating with each other, held a council in a place appointed, to which they invited men of wisdom and experience. The conclusion they came to was this: "The Ottoman Emperor having introduced an admirable system into his army, and established a corps for the express purpose of keeping it up, we shall no longer be able to keep face with such well disciplined troops: as the soldiers of the Islam are naturally brave, they will fall in among us, sword in hand, and make a speedy end of us; and as the opinion which they hold that those who die in war are martyrs, and go immediately to Paradise, makes them fight with great zeal, it is evident that if we do not establish good and sufficient military regulations, the Ottomans will conquer the whole of Europe, and oblige us all to pay the Haratsh. It is our business therefore to find some method of preventing those soldiers from closing with us." They concluded their conference by forming a masterly project, and inventing a method of using with expedition their cannon, muskets, and other instruments of war, and prohibiting their troops from engaging in commerce, they obliged them to pass their whole time in learning military exercises, in which they made such progress that it became at last impossible to break their ranks. In truth, it is well known to those who are acquainted with history, that in the wars which have taken place since the invention of this new system of tactics, the Ottomans have been most frequently worsted, because they found it impossible to make use of their sabres among the infidels as they wished to do; for their regular troops keep in a compact body, pressing their feet together that their order of battle may not be broken; and their cannon being polished like one of[86]Marcovich's watches, they load twelve times in a minute, and make the bullets rain like musket balls; thus they keep up an unintermitted discharge of artillery and small arms. When the Islamites make an attack upon them with infantry or cavalry, the enemies of our faith observe a profound silence, till the soldiers of Islam are come close up to their front, and then at once giving fire to some hundred carriage-guns, and to seventy or eighty thousand muskets, overturn our men in heaps without so much as receiving a bloody nose. When they have thus by a few volleys caused thousands of the people of Islam to drink the sherbet of martyrdom, the surviving remnant are wont to fly. Our troops perceiving how skilful the enemy are in the use of fire-arms, and seeing many thousand men slain in the space of half an hour, while they are unable to avenge themselves on their opponents, have necessarily begun to lose courage. But although the wicked infidels, exerting their whole strength, have with great prudence and boldness invented so masterly an art of war, yet the soldiers of Islam, who have not been able to make any stand against them, may justly assert that the fault does not belong to themselves; for since the enemy sends us eighty thousand charges of grape before a thousand of our men have time to fire their muskets, it is certain that resistance in such a case is beyond their power. Thus during the period which elapsed before the reign of his Highness Sultan Mustapha Khan, although we were sometimes victorious and sometimes vanquished, yet success was, for the most part, on the side of the infidels.

By explaining all this, and by giving answers founded on the knowledge of passing events, I have succeeded in convincing many persons, who by falsehood endeavoured to support the unjust opposition of the partisans of the Janissaries. What remains to be mentioned is this: His Highness Sultan Mahmoud, having enquired the reason of the successes of the infidels, and the defeats of the people of Islam, a dissertation, treating of the way to victory, and entitled "The Origin of Discipline," was composed and published; and as it afforded satisfaction to the Emperor, copies of it were disseminated amongst the public. I have, in the year 1206, undertaken to write a description of the new troops, being encouraged thereto by the favour which the Emperor has been pleased to bestow both on the motive and the work; but as, by the mercy of Heaven, I have reached the extreme period of life, it is very uncertain whether I shall be able to finish the execution of it.

SECTION IV.

"Since you cannot reconcile your minds to the new system of exercise, and say that it is useless, allow me in reply to put this question to you: Was there a wall run up between you and the infidels during the Russian war which broke out in the reign of Sultan Mustapha Khan? When you had consumed as much meat and white bread as would have been sufficient for two hundred thousand men, why did you, while the infidels were in your sight, turn and fly, instead of engaging them after you had raised a commotion on the pay, rations, and exceptions from service? You well know that I was present with you at that time. In the following year you committed, on your march to the army, sundry crimes and excesses; burning and ruining the houses in which you were lodged, both of Mussulmans and tributary subjects, and lengthening your hands against their children and daughters. When you arrived at the camp, you plainly showed what ability you possessed for war, never having ventured in any situation to engage or oppose the enemy, even so much as with the sound of your voices; and after having spent your time as you did the former year, in disputing about pay, &c. you departed, spoiling your brothers in religion, and showing no fear or reverence, either for God or man. Prove to us, if you can, that at any time, or in any place, you have rendered the least service to the Emperor. Such being the state you were in for the space of six or seven years, you at length became the cause of the Muscovites concluding a treaty with us on their own terms, inasmuch as through your misconduct they were enabled to penetrate into our territories. And to conclude all, it is owing to you that such a province as the Crimea, the seat of a Khan, hath remained in the hands of the infidels.—In the late war with the Russians, which followed the one we have been speaking of, several thousand soldiers of the corps of the Janissaries were detached with speed on the side of Otchakow, with the hope that you would effect something before the military forces of the Russians could arrive from a distance of seven or eight hundred hours' march.[87] On that occasion you paid no attention to your officers or to the governor of Otchakow, but of your own counsel went to attack a little entrenched port called Kibburun, where, being engaged by a small body of Russian troops appointed to defend that quarter, you could not resist them, but returned to Otchakow, after losing a great number of men. The Muscovites then besieged the fortress of Otchakow, remaining before it during the season of winter, snow, and extreme cold, whilst you crept into holes within the place, and did not dare to venture out. Thus you were the occasion of the enemy's taking by assault, and by force of arms, so strong and firm a bulwark of Islamism, together with all its inhabitants, who were made prisoners. And to you it is owing that so many thousand persons, with their wives, daughters, and young children, fell into the hands of the Russians. In other places you were equally unable to resist. As the superiority which the practice of military exercise gives to the infidels in war is clearly evident, as well as the deficiency of the people of Islam in several points connected with military science, is not the obstinacy with which you oppose the introduction of this exercise, purely a treason against our religion and empire?" When I had thus set forth and laid before them their actual condition, such of them as were disposed to reason ceased their clamour, and answered thus: "Truly His Highness Sultan Mahmoud was about to appoint a deputation for the purpose of establishing this exercise, according to the principles laid down in the treatise entitled 'The Origin of the Institution of Discipline;' but as longer life was not granted to him, the deputation was not named. If at that period good order had been established, we should not have been beaten by the infidels." In these words they made confession of the truth; but some answered differently, saying, "In the corps of Janissaries I receive twenty-five aspers; if these troops of the Nizam-y-Gedid should increase in number, and become serviceable, I am afraid that as the Janissaries will no longer enjoy any consideration, I shall not be able to draw my pay. If I knew for certain that no loss would accrue to me from it, I would say, God grant that all the people in the world may become soldiers of the Nizam-y-Gedid." These people expressed their true sentiments. Others again spoke thus: "If we abolish the new regulation (although we know that it is likely to be serviceable, and that our other undisciplined forces will never be of the least avail) the enemy will celebrate the event with the rejoicings of a marriage-feast, and encroaching on our territories more and more, will confirm their victory by imposing on the Sublime Government hard and disgraceful conditions; and to conclude, as there will be no means of opposing the enemies of our faith on any side, the power of the Sublime Government will decline from day to day. If, under the Divine favour, these troops who are clothed with the garments of discipline, should be augmented until they amount to the number required, and stationed in the fortresses upon the Russian and German frontiers, as well as in other parts of the empire, we very well know that, in a time of trouble and of war, they will not be disconcerted like our raw soldiers, but will stand firm and unshaken in the midst of carnage. We will prove the truth of our words by this example: If, on a stormy day, a vessel be manned with persons utterly ignorant of sea affairs, the ship will undoubtedly sink, and all on board will perish; but if the crew are acquainted with navigation, however great may be the storm which they encounter, they will, by the grace of God, obtain a deliverance from it. Can there be any room to doubt that a few persons who have for fifteen or twenty years exercised the art of war, and have learnt sundry military stratagems, will obtain an easy victory over many thousand unpractised soldiers, overthrowing them, and bringing them into captivity?" In such terms as these many of them avowed their assent and conviction. It ought to be generally known that, whilst many thousands of our undisciplined forces were unable to obtain the least advantage in the war which they waged at Alexandria and Cairo against the reprobates of France, our gunners and regular infantry, although few in number, bravely combating the infidels and defeated them incessantly; and the flight of a single individual of that corps was never seen nor heard of. As their valour was conspicuous to all, many of those who had carped at them saw and acknowledged their error, saying "these are the troops who will render effectual service, and we have sinned in calumniating them." His Highness Gezar-Pashah seeing the greatness of soul which these men displayed in war, and with what heroic courage they became martyrs, while not a single individual thought of flight, spoke thus: "Truly before I knew what sort of men these were, I was wont to abuse them; but if after this I do so again, may my tongue be dried in my mouth." This we have heard from persons who were present at the time that he said it. If we possess any understanding or sense of rectitude, and be able to distinguish good from evil, we may perceive and comprehend how important and necessary the services of these troops have been; and also that, with the exception of this sort of regular soldiers, the residue of our forces have only served to create confusion and occasion famine, in our camps, frontier fortresses, and other military posts. There are certain expressions current amongst the enemies of our faith which our ears heard in the time of our captivity. They say thus: "The greater is the number of troops sent by the Ottomans into the field, the better are we pleased; because if they are very numerous, their magazines will be exhausted, and they will disperse before two months have passed; and if your raw soldiers march against us, the greater part of them will be mowed down by our grape shot, and the remainder will fly." Behold, we have seen with our eyes that this saying is exactly conformable to truth. The following is another of their expressions: "If, for instance, in an army of one hundred thousand Ottomans, there could be found an hundred well trained men, we should, in computing their numbers, only reckon those hundred, without taking the others into our calculation, because we know that one soldier thoroughly exercised, is equal to one thousand raw and ignorant men." It is a certain fact, that we have seen in the wars persons who, having never in the course of their lives taken a gun in their hands before, but spent all their time in the exercise of some trade, and knew not what they were about, but first put the ball into their muskets, and then the powder above it. It has been sometimes proved by experience, that as these people know not how to handle their ammunition, it would be better that they should leave the army rather than remain with it; because, being of no use, they do harm by the disorder which they create. Some of our raw soldiers who do not know the proper charge of powder, by putting too great a quantity into their guns, cause them to burst, and thus maim, or even kill both themselves and those who stand near them; and many of our unpractised horsemen who, when mounted on their steeds, fancy themselves the heroes of the age, and would not deign to give a salutation even to their own fathers, when they draw their sabres in action, wound the heads of their own horses, and thus cover themselves and their beasts with blood; this awkwardness of theirs cause those who see it to utter ejaculations of surprise. In short, it is evident to men of understanding, that as the talents of reading, writing, riding on horseback, shooting with the bow, playing on an instrument, and other similar acquirements, will not come spontaneously to persons unskilled, and uninstructed in them; so likewise victory cannot be obtained without a knowledge of the art of war, which is a particular, and noble branch of science, independent of others.

There are indeed certain considerations which may induce us to pardon those calumniators of the Nizam-y-Gedid, who are any wise connected with the old corps; but do those persons who are by no means attached to them, and who know the difference between alum and[88]sugar, and between good and evil, show any sense in daring to abuse so noble a science? Their perverseness and obstinacy are astonishing, seeing that, notwithstanding the taste which the infidel race has always had of our raw troops, they do not allow it to be sufficiently proved, that if a war should break out, these ignorant beasts pressing together in masses of one or two thousand men, will be unable to resist the tactic of the enemy.

SECTION V.
Containing a relation of the footing on which the old corps of troops originally were, and of their present state.

Since so unreasonable a dissension prevails between our old and new troops, we have undertaken a disquisition on the organization of the first of these corps. The public are well aware of the conduct observed by our old corps of troops when they march out to war, or return from it; but if any persons should be ignorant of this, we will thus explain it to them. At the time that His Highness Sultan Suleÿman Khan set on foot these forces, the soldiers whose names were inscribed on the muster-roll conducted themselves on their marches with the most perfect propriety; and at the places through which they passed, whether they moved by land or by water, did not take so much as the value of an asper, either from rich or poor, mussulman or Rayah; neither did they eat a single egg without paying for it, nor injured the honour of any one. Truly the said troops, yielding implicit obedience to the orders of the emperor of the times, and of their other commanders, performed their duty well, and wronged no man in any respect. In their military expeditions they were wont to subdue forts and countries, and to ruin the reputation of the infidels, and thus to elevate the glory, fame, and power of the emperor of exalted splendour, and as they were thought worthy of the prayers of his Highness and of the people of the true faith, the whole world held them as objects of praise, and all men desired their honour. As they were so highly respected a body, they did not admit into their ranks men of obscure race, such as Franks, Greeks, Armenians, Jews, or gypsies, or persons belonging to any other inglorious nation. Being men of true courage, they repressed these as well as all other insolent and shameless persons, and those of the description of robbers. As the enemies of our religion were not pleased with their excellent regulations, they found means to introduce into their ranks very cunning spies for the purpose of sowing dissension amongst them. These spies gradually creeping in amongst the soldiers under pretence of being comrades, insinuated themselves like Satan, and began by degrees to set on foot practices, tending to corrupt the valour implanted in their hearts, and their zeal for religion. "Comrades (said they) the pay which we receive from government is seven aspers, and they point out to us Paradise as the reward of martyrdom; they will certainly cause us all to be slaughtered by the infidels; we have not two lives, why then should we be destroyed for seven aspers, and without reason?" Having, by similar and repeated insinuations, corrupted the minds of the faithful soldiers, these began to care no longer about the concerns they were intended for, and saying at last, "Useless and destructive expeditions are only proper for the Russian infidels, let us leave it to their soldiers to feed upon dry biscuits, as for us we will return home and eat fine Baklava."[89] Thus they forgot the stream of benefits in which they were immersed, and the kind treatment and protection that they had experienced. As there was nobody, either in the corps or out of it, who spoke reason to them, they came in process of time to do whatever they liked, plundering the places that they traversed on their march, burning and destroying the houses both of Mussulmans and Rayahs, and stretching forth their hands against the honour of their families. Besides all this, although the whole body of men who compose an hundred and ninety six Ortas, being quartered altogether in one residence, ought to have no differences one with the other; yet hatred and dissension rose to such a pitch amongst them, that they no longer considered those who did not belong to their own Orta, as brothers in religion, but, without dissembling their sentiments, exchanged bullets, and drank each others blood; and in the villages, forcing open the houses of the poor, committed murder, which disorder still prevailing, as none of them are safe from the others either in war or peace, their well regulated system of discipline hath perished and gone to decay. They pass their days in propagating seventy thousand false reports, saying, "When we were opposed to the infidels, they did not allow us to give them battle; if we had obtained permission, we could without trouble have overthrown the crals from their thrones; but the ministers of our government conspiring with the Ghiaours[90] cause us to be slain and taken prisoners, and, receiving from the Russian infidels casks of gold, deliver up the country to them."

On a day of battle, as soon as they have heard from a distance the noise of a cannonade, and have seen a few hats, the Mussulman spies who are in their ranks begin to exclaim aloud: "Community of Mahomet, why do you stay here? the Ghiaours have forced our camp, the troops in front of us have turned their faces this way; we shall be pursued and made prisoners." As these cries spread in succession through the army, even the very regiments which since their original institution never surrendered their kettles to the enemy[91], and which are at that moment sacrificing a thousand martyrs in their defence, now estimating their own lives at the price which the others set upon theirs, abandon in the space of half an hour their tents, camp equipage, kettles, and baggage of every sort, and repairing straight to the imperial camp, plunder the treasure, effects, and military chest, and then adorning their heads with the trophies of their pillage, walk about in small parties with a presumptuous air, as though these were inscriptions which made good their pretence of having beaten the enemy, and overturned their cral. As they are all mixed and confounded together, there is no way of distinguishing those who fight with true patriotism from those who do not, and there are amongst them certain adversaries who begin the attack against the orders of their Vezier, Agha, Pashahs, and other officers. When, however, the action is engaged, it is not possible to make them stand their ground for half a minute, and the following example is a clear proof of it. During the reign of his Highness Sultan Moustapha, in the year of the battle of Kartal, when an hundred and fifty thousand soldiers of Islam were opposed to the infidels, whilst his excellency, Cogia Abdee Pashah (who hath attained to the mercy of God,) was engaged in combat on the field of battle, at which time the people of Islam were not very hard pressed, a mounted spy, dressed like a Chiaoush, rode hastily along the rear of the entrenchments of the Janissaries, and cried aloud: "Janissaries, why do you remain here? the Ghiaours have turned our rear!" having said these words, he put spurs to his horse and departed. Before he was out of sight, the whole camp of janissaries, without examining whether he had spoken truth or falsehood, at once betook themselves to a precipitate flight. The infidels, availing themselves of the opportunity, pursued them, and were on the point of completing their destruction; but his excellency, whom we mentioned above, saved them by vigorously charging the infidels with another corps; but while he thus checked the enemy, the fugitives never thought so much as rallying or coming to his assistance, neither did they stop to take breath, until they arrived on the banks of the Danube, amongst the tents which contained the treasure. As they did not see the enemy at their backs, they ought to have retraced their steps, instead of which, they plundered the baggage and treasure of the imperial camp, and not being able to cross the river in open boats, they threw themselves into the river, so that one third of them, or perhaps more, were swallowed up in the Danube. Some, who could not swim, climbed up the willow-trees upon the banks of the Danube, and many lay hid among the reeds and flags; but when the enemy arrived and perceived them, they were all put to death by fire and sword. It was exactly three days before the whole army of the infidels came up, when they made themselves masters of all the artillery, ammunition, and military stores of various descriptions, which our bravoes, who were unable to carry them off, had left on the banks of the Danube.

Towards the conclusion of the Russian war, which had succeeded the one we have been speaking of, when Cogia Jussuf Pashah was Grand Vezier for the second time, all the officers of the corps, and the Janissary-Agha coming up to the Vezier in a body, made to him this representation: "Although we have upwards of one hundred and twenty thousand men, yet eight thousand of the Russian troops, crossing to the higher side of the Danube and attacking us, have completely routed our army. It is utterly impossible for us, with our regular troops, to make head against such welldisciplined forces as those of the Ghiaours; therefore, if you intend to make peace with them, do it without delay. While our soldiers continue ignorant of these new military manœuvres, we are not destined to become victorious, from this time even to the day of judgment." The astonished Vezier said in answer to this strong representation, "How can I lay these points before the Emperor?" To this they replied, "We will ourselves cause a petition to be drawn up and presented to him." At the same time, they caused an humble representation to be written out by me, and delivered it to the Vezier. It was dispatched to the Emperor, and his Highness became convinced of their inability of obtaining success in future. When peace was made, in consequence, the Sublime Government, considering that the Janissaries themselves had declared that their state of discipline rendered them unfit to oppose the tactics of the enemies, thought itself obliged to use every effort to introduce into the corps of Janissaries a regular system of exercise, hoping by that means to retrieve their affairs, to avert defeat, to open the way to victory, and to obtain security from hostile machinations. The Janissaries, however, contrary to reason and expectation, would not receive this project, and absolutely rejected it. But as it became evident that, if it were abandoned to oblivion, things would become worse, and the infidel race would certainly encroach more and more, and as the conversation which had taken place at Petersburgh relative to the reservoirs, was then generally known, a body of musketeers was formed from among the Bostangees, and quartered in the barracks newly constructed at the Levend-Chifflick. As when His Highness Sultan Suleÿman set on foot the corps of Janissaries, the new recruits deserted next day, so in the present instance a number of worthless persons set up an opposition in defence of the Janissaries, although these were no otherwise connected with it than by the simple reception of pay, and began to whisper to each other, "Hark ye! a hearth[92] is set open for the Nizam-y-Gedid; if these new troops, who are practising military evolutions, should perform any good service in war, the institution of Janissaries will become obsolete, and our muster-roll will be erased from the list." They suggested also, that as the men who were inscribed in the corps of the Nizam-y-Gedid performed an exercise similar to that of the Ghiaours, the Mussulman faith is thereby injured. Although these blockheads had never before given themselves any concern about our faith or government, and indeed knew nothing of what belongs to Mussulman purity; yet, on the present occasion, they showed a mighty anxiety for religion, and by that means prevented many persons from inscribing their names, and encouraged many who were already engaged to desert. Behold! how inscrutable are the decrees of Divine Providence! When the war with France broke out, at which time these forces consisted only of three or four thousand men, the new gunners and musketeers were appointed to serve at Cairo and Acre. The said troops committed no excesses, either on board the vessels in which they were transported, or in the places of their destination whither they repaired, nor robbed any man of the value of an asper; but both in going and coming, conducted themselves with propriety and modesty. If any persons have either seen or heard of their having committed the least fault, we challenge them to declare it. When by the favour of Divine Providence they arrived at Acre, the French infidels, who had for sixty-three days pressed very closely Gezar-Pashah and the inhabitants of the place, were within a hair's breadth of making themselves entirely masters of it; for they had already entered that which is called the Sublime bastion within the fortress; but the troops of the Nizam-y-Gedid, valiantly exerting their military skill, in one day slaughtered the infidels to such a degree, that in no part of Europe did the French nation ever receive so disgraceful an overthrow; and no man in the world is ignorant that the said fortress and its inhabitants were delivered by their courage. Is not this also a proof of their utility, past and future? Wherever they have been opposed to the infidels, although few in number, they never turned their faces back, but broke the enemy, or were themselves broken; and as not one of them dared to mention the word flight, they have always, in exact obedience to the will of the great and mighty Prophet, punctually discharged the duties which appertain to a holy war, and a steady zeal for the faith. If there is any falsehood in my words, let any one prove it; I am extremely willing that he should do so, otherwise, for God's sake, let every body listen to reason. When our undisciplined forces in Egypt found themselves unable to make head against the cavalry or infantry of the French infidels, they retired for protection behind the ranks of our regular troops, who alone stood their ground, and by that means saved themselves from the impending danger. Moreover, in the year 1217 they were sent against the Mountaineers who had rebelled in Rumelia. Since that insolent race first showed themselves, several Veziers and other officers had been sent against them without effect.[93] Having formed the wicked design of destroying the Nizam-y-Gedid institution from its roots, they now exerted their whole strength and gave battle. Although the regular troops had with them neither their cannon, howitzers, or mounted men, and were engaged in the midst of a severe winter, snow, rain, and mud, and though the rebels were strongly posted in a town, they nevertheless marched up to the attack, and without regarding the advantageous position of the insurgents, while they were themselves up to the knees in mud and water, they knocked down half of the rebels like rotten pears, sending their souls to hell, and obliged the rest to fly. In a short time the field of action was covered with the vile carcases of the rebels, and those who were taken alive reported that they called out to each other, "Ah! comrade, these troops which they call Nizam-y-Gedid, are not what we took them for." In these exclamations they betrayed the sense of their own inferiority. Every one knows that at last these rascals, unable to make a stand on any side, climbed the mountains by night, and fled. To this we may add, that although the banditti tried by every means to introduce a spy into the ranks of the new soldiers, they could not succeed, because, by the regulations of those forces, an officer is appointed to command every ten privates, and these officers who have an opportunity of seeing constantly, as well their own men as those who are on the right and left, are acquainted with them all, and in the line they never quit each other's sides; if, therefore, a stranger from without should get in amongst them, in what condition would he find himself, being exposed in the middle; like a broom in a court-yard, he delivers his collar to the first man that takes him.

Just and intelligent men may readily understand how easily the Sublime Government can organise these troops, from this circumstance, that it is utterly impossible for any person, whether Mussulman or infidel, by passing to and fro to examine the state of these troops, and learn where they are going, and what they are about to undertake, without being discovered and punished. The advantages of the new corps, and their superiority over the old are infinite; were we to write them all down, we should fill several volumes. In order, however, to make the people comprehend well, we will point out to them another of these advantages. The soldiers of our ancient corps, are not at all clothed alike; from this diversity of garment, the following bad effect results: if, in time of war, any of them should desert from the army, as there are no marks by which we can distinguish whether the deserters belong to the troops, or whether they are tradesmen, or servants, they have thereby the opportunities of escaping without being known. Whereas the new troops have a particular uniform of their own, so that the stragglers would be soon discovered. Hence it results, that in a large camp of the new troops, every man will be forced to remain fixed in his company, and steady in the performance of his duty, whether he would or no, since it is impossible to desert without greatly incurring the danger of punishment.

Another of their advantages is this: our old forces, when in presence of the enemy, do not remain drawn up in a line, but stand confusedly and promiscuously like a crowd in a place of diversion. Some load their muskets, and fire once, some twice, or oftener, just as they think proper, whilst others being at their wits' end, and not knowing what they are about turn from side to side like fabulous story-tellers.[94] If in consequence of any movement which they perceive on the side of the enemy, the officers endeavour to make the troops fall back a little, some will obey them, others will not, every one does just as he likes. If they wish to retire a little, the soldiers make that a pretence for flying to the distance of some days' journey.

But the new troops remain drawn up in line as though they were at prayers, the rear ranks being exactly parallel with the front, and consisting of the same number of companies, neither more nor less, so that, when it is necessary, they turn with as much precision as a watch. The whole body, consisting of many thousand men, observe attentively the signals given them by the two fuglemen who explain by signs the commands of the officers, and not one dares so much as to turn his head. Thus the orders of the officers being communicated without the least noise, they stand firm, and lend an attentive ear, whilst not a word issues from their mouths. If, for instance, the officer whose business it is to give the command, makes the signal for attention, the whole body are ready in an instant, and not one of them dares to stand idle, or to make any noise, or to look another way, thus they are equally prepared for whatever may happen. Sometimes the signal is given for them to load and discharge their muskets successively, without regarding order or slacken their fire, so as to make the balls shower like rain. If, while thus engaged, they meet with a check, the officers immediately by a signal will cause them to retire in good order, and will supply their place with fresh troops from the rear, who likewise scatter their fire in the same manner. This method of managing troops gives great facility to their operations. Sometimes they dispose a large body of men in a circular form, and then cause them to march round in such a manner, that as the circle turns the soldiers incessantly discharge their muskets on the enemy and give no respite to the combat, and having prepared their guns for a fresh discharge before they return to the same place, they fire the moment they arrive in the face of the enemy. The result of this circular formation is, that the fire and slaughter do not cease for an instant. Sometimes, when it is judged necessary, several thousand men being crowded into a narrow space, form a solid mass for the purpose of appearing to the enemy to be few in number, then by opening out, they can execute any manœuvre that they please, and sometimes, ten thousand men deploying, appear to consist of fifty or sixty thousand. At other times, when they are hard pressed, the troops receive the superior officers in the centre, and throwing themselves into the form of a square castle, pour their fire on every side, the artillery also being disposed on every face of the square, so that if the enemy should charge them even on four sides, he will be unable to make an impression. If the enemy's cavalry should endeavour to break in upon them while they are formed in this manner, on the signal being given, the front rank men kneel altogether in an instant, and remain in that position keeping their muskets supported against their breasts, and the ranks who are in their rear stand upright and make use of their fire-arms, thus rendering it impossible for the hostile cavalry to break in and create confusion. Should it happen that the enemy is as skilful and well trained as themselves, and employs against them the same discipline, then of the two parties, that will be victorious whose chiefs are enabled, by the favour of Divine Providence, to put in practice with superior address, the new science and stratagems of war which they have learned, because the apostle of the Most High, our great prophet (on whom be the blessings and peace of God!) himself condescended to use military stratagems. This sacred tradition is thus related.

During a holy war which was carried on in the happy time of the apostle of God, (on whom be peace!) a certain valiant champion of the enemy's army came out to offer single combat, and demanded that the glorious Alli should be opposed to him. Alli, well pleasing to God, having received the command of the Apostle, girded on his sword only, and immediately went forth alone to the place appointed for the combat. When this friend of the Most High met that infidel, he thus addressed him: "I come on foot having one sword; why come you out on horseback having two swords and two bows?" The great Alli spoke to him again, saying "let these things be so; but I come out alone to give battle on our side, why do you bring another man and come both together?" The infidel, at this question, looked about him believing that another man had followed him, when at the same instant, the great Alli, in the twinkling of an eye, made the vile head of the reprobate fly off. The death of the said wicked person having been a source of joy to the followers of Islam, the excellent Alli, meeting the great prophet on his return, related to him the admirable stratagem by means of which he had slain that wretch. This holy tradition has been vouchsafed unto us.

Although many similar stratagems have been employed at various times, by holy warriors, and leave has been granted to the spies sent forth amongst the infidels for the purpose of advancing victory to the people of Islam, to assume any sort of dress; and although the great Prophet hath given full permission and authority to do any thing which may conduce to the defeat of the infidels, yet an ignorant rabble keep chattering like parrots, some of whom do not approve of the dresses of the new troops, while others say that their exercise belongs specially to the Kiafers[95], and does not become Mussulmans.

With respect to the manner in which the provinces of the Sublime Government are to be defended, and the means by which the enemies of our faith are to be repressed, and the causes that have produced victory and defeat, the rabble are utterly ignorant of them, occupying themselves solely with this question, "shall we lose our pay of a few aspers?" With this, as with a fishing hook, they draw from their sack various absurdities, and prevent a number of simple and foolish men from undertaking the duties of holy warfare. In truth, is not this a sufficient reason for their being excluded from the two blessed worlds?

To sum up all in one word: it is evident to men of penetration, that there is no possibility of introducing this system into our old corps, for this reason; that as at their first institution they were regulated in a different manner, every one of them has an aversion to submitting himself to the new discipline. If, for example, any of the old troops wish to leave the camp and return, although forty thousand officers should attempt to turn them back, it is useless; they will do as they please. If only five or ten individuals should turn their faces, who has power to say to them "Stop, go not away!" the whole body forthwith following on their steps; for the most part draws breath in the tents containing the treasure and baggage of the Imperial camp.

The following is another of the advantages of the new troops. If it should happen that the enemies have obtained the victory by their superior numbers, and that the new forces were defeated, they will not, in consequence, lose courage and disperse themselves; their captains and other officers will rally them the following day or soon after, and will again march upon the enemy; and not one of their soldiers will dare to make the defeat a pretext for quitting his post. But if our old corps meet with a small check, they run, throw themselves into the water, and get drowned. Thus they become the cause of the progress of the enemies of the faith. Which thing having come to pass in our own times, twice in the Russian, and once in the Austrian war, and repeatedly in the war with the French, is manifest to the world, and wants no new proof.[96] Another of the advantages of the new troops is this; that when a body of them are appointed to defend any post, they establish an advanced guard round the place in order to obviate any hostile stratagems. Although this sort of vigilance and precaution was formerly observed, yet there is a world of difference between the ancient method and the new. According to the old system, it is not easy to discover strange soldiers of the enemies' army who mix with the posts; but it is utterly impossible for strangers to pass the guards of the regular troops, and to get into a fortress which they defend; so that the army is safe from any surprise.

The following is a description of the manner in which these posts are arranged. When they are disposed round the camp, a certain word is given them every night as a sign; the commander-in-chief first announces in secret this word to the officers, and they communicate it privately to the officers of the corps de garde; if therefore they meet with a suspicious person, they immediately demand the parole, that is to say, the sign word for the night; and if he does not give the parole of the night, they seize and conduct him to the captain of the camp. Behold! this is the only method of discovering spies; and as it is a matter which, above all others, demands great care, they will pay special attention to it; so that until their return from any expedition, the parole of one night will never be the same as that of another, and by this means they are delivered from the plague of spies. But of all the advantages, the most material is this. If, under Divine favour, a sufficiently numerous body of these new troops should be properly disposed along the frontiers of the Sublime Empire, our enemies will find themselves opposed on every part of the boundaries of Islam, by expert artillery men, and well disciplined forces, perfectly acquainted with the rules of the art of war; nor will they, as heretofore, be able to take advantage of our unguarded posture, in order to make an attack upon us; for there are persons still alive who well know that when in the time of Sultan Mahmoud the German infidels assaulted, and at once made themselves masters of the fortress of Nissa, it required a great deal of trouble to drive them out. In fine, His Highness the Emperor, and the supporters of his power, considering that it is indispensably necessary to guard against such occurrences by striking terror into the enemies of our religion, have firmly resolved to take measures for that purpose, seeing that those enemies who were from the beginning a troublesome and insolent race, and who, in all times, had been unable to withstand the power of the people of Islam, insomuch that they were wont to frighten their bastards in the cradle by saying "The Mussulman is coming!" and many of them on seeing one Mussulman, took off their hats through excess of fear, now venture to resist us, and have with exceeding care and diligence made themselves so thoroughly masters of the use of fire-arms, that a body of some thousands of them are able to serve their cannon with as much precision and celerity as they can their muskets, firing a single piece of artillery twelve or fifteen times in a minute, and making a thousand discharges in the space of an hour. By this means they destroy the people of Islam from a distance, and prevent them from making use of their sabres. They now say, "At length we have taught the Ottoman troops what value they ought to set upon themselves; henceforth they will never set foot in our country; even the Mussulman provinces are ours." Thus they never allow victory to incline to the side of Islam, and especially since the year 1182, they have continued to afflict the followers of Islam with most disgraceful usage, bringing under their own power so many of our tributary subjects. Nevertheless, a crowd of ignorant people of our nation never bring these things into their recollection, nor can persuade themselves that the success of the infidels for nearly the space of forty years over the people of Islam proceeds entirely from their own inability to resist their fire, and that their own frequent flights are the cause which disables us from carrying on war. These despicable wretches have never issued from the castle-gate, nor travelled a single stage from home, neither do they know what war and peace mean, nor from what cause the troubles of the world have sprung, and whence they are likely to arise in future; some of them are so ignorant of what belongs to pure religion, that in repeating a short prayer they commit mistakes from beginning to end; men in appearance only, vulgar of the lowest description, children of falsehood, who suppose that the Nizam-y-Gedid is the cause of confusion in the universe, and that if this ordinance were removed, and the old system restored, the world would be tranquil in five days.

Last year, one of those superlatively ignorant persons was appointed to the office of receiver of the revenue in one of the islands. This man, who before was continually uttering curses and execrations against the authors of the Nizam-y-Gedid, having gained five thousand piasters by the perception of the imposts, and hoping it was continued to him for another year that he might gain five thousand more, upon meeting with his friends and companions, said to them, "Ha! comrades, there is no harm in this Nizam-y-Gedid; I, indeed, at first opposed it, but it was from want of sense; for the impost upon wine is not paid by those who drink it, but is levied upon the wine which is sent to Russia, so that the money comes out of the pockets of the Russians; it were better that it was twice as much; I now understand the matter, and I make vow never to speak a word against the Nizam-y-Gedid." See how this man, in consequence of gaining a few piasters by an institution which he had been in the habit of abusing, is not ashamed afterwards to praise it. Such, however, is the nature of all the lower orders. To sum up all in one word: if the clamour and execrations of a rabble, who makes no difference between good and evil, obliges us to abandon the said institution of new troops, (which Heaven forbid!) the enemies of our religion will find so much the more facility in invading us; and as one of their kingdoms maintains three hundred thousand regular troops, they will mount upon our necks on seeing that the Ottomans cannot discipline a hundred thousand. At that time we shall not derive the least service from those knaves who disapprove of the Nizam-y-Gedid; they will merely say that it was thus ordained; that there is no contending with destiny; and if a great calamity befalls (which Heaven avert!) they will, without making more words about the matter, become the authors of trouble and distress.

SECTION VI.
Wherein is explained the purpose for which exercise is intended.

In the time of his Highness the late Emperor, during the period of my two captivities, I have often, in the course of conversation with Russian military men, questioned them, saying, "by what secret prodigy hath it come to pass, that you Muscovites, who were formerly a very stupid and easily vanquished nation, have for some time back obtained such success over the race of Osman?" They, in reply, said, "Since you are ignorant of the causes of our superiority, you shall be made acquainted with them. The Russians, in former times, did not possess the knowledge of tactics, and were therefore beaten by their enemies. A man called Mad [97]Petro, having in his travels seen the world, and acquired an intimate knowledge of the advantages thereof, became Cral of Muscovy, and subjected the Russians, whether they would or no, to the restraints of discipline. In order to try what progress they had made in it, he declared war against the King of Sweden, and avenged himself of him. He then went in an expedition towards the Crimea, reduced whatever fortresses he thought proper, and began to break the power of the Tartars. Afterwards, when we concluded a treaty with you, we demanded for our Cral the title of Emperor; and as you could not oppose us, the Sultan Mahmoud Khan (of excellent memory) in writing to us, granted that title. Then in the war with Sultan Moustapha, we approached Adrianople, and made peace on our own terms. And see, in the present war, we have, with very few troops, defeated your numerous forces; and after taking the fortresses of Hotim, Bender, Ibraïl, Ismail, and Otchakoff, and conquering Moldavia and Wallachia from one extremity to the other, we passed the Danube with eight thousand men, and routed the Ottoman army consisting of fifty thousand. As you have no troops able to face ours, know that this time also, after being well beaten, you will make a worse peace than the former one." In this manner did they answer this poor person[98]; and truly before much time had elapsed, it came to pass that such a treaty was concluded.

SECTION VII.

It is a difficult thing to find out the spies that go to and fro in the camps of the followers of Islam, and it is necessary to explain how much injury is done by them. As this matter requires attention above all others, let us relate some events which have happened to us, with the consequences resulting from them.

In the war with the Russians, during the reign of the late Emperor, Sultan Moustapha, two hundred thousand unknown and undisciplined troops were drawn together. In this multitude no one knew the other, and if a father had searched for his own son, he could not have found him. If each day some hundreds separated themselves and went off, no one knew it, nor even could have said to them, 'stop! remain!' In so disorderly a camp, the spies from the side of the infidels came and went each day and night, and acquainted the Russians with every thing that passed in our army, and the secrets of our government became known to the enemy. For this reason, whenever a forward movement of our army was resolved upon, they surprised the camp towards morning, the day before it was to be executed, and routed so large an army of the Ottoman race, without allowing them to open their eyes, all being buried in sleep. We have learned by experience, that as the infidel race are very cunning and deceitful, they have often effected, merely by wiles and stratagems, things which we never have been, nor ever will be, able to bring about with our hundred thousand men. Among all the wiles which that wicked race have put in practice, there is one extraordinary stratagem which it is worth while for us to describe. During the said war, three poor men belonging to the assembly of Janissaries, having concerted together, went out to gain some information of the Russians: after it was quite dark they seized, on the Muscovite borders, a certain Ghiaour, one of those who were employed in getting forage, and, satisfied with their success, were conducting him to the camp, when, their prisoner being a cunning hog[99] that understood Turkish, said to them, "Sirs! if you set me at liberty, my father, who is a rich man, will recompense you largely." They, believing his words, conducted him back to the Russian confines, where he soon found a surreptitious pimp[99] whom he called father, to whom they delivered him. This man, who was also a very deceitful rogue, said to them, "I am greatly pleased at your bringing my son here and not killing him, and I am very much obliged to you." With these and other expressions of gratitude, he gave them five ducats, and continued thus: "I have not been able to reward you as I ought to do, but allow me to show you something, and let that be another recompense." So saying, he carried them in disguise into his own camp, and placed them at the edge of a large tent; here the comrades perceived that there was a great bustle before the tent, and that within they were weighing gold and silver coin in a large balance, and were then filling with it some casks placed near. In the tent were men habited in divers sorts of Mussulman dresses, and the casks filled with money were continually distributed amongst them. The traitor, after showing these things to the three comrades, took them to his own tent, and said to them, "Comrades! see what I have shown you. Part of this money is to go to your government, and part to the Vezier and other Generals of your army. We have purchased your country with money; the sum that has just been given is the price of Constantinople which we have bought and shall soon enter. My motive for informing you of this is that you may henceforth look to yourselves; do not remain in your camp, nor even lose time at Constantinople; but go to your own country that you may not be made prisoners. Keep all this secret, and say nothing of it in your camp." With these words he led them back to the Ottoman confines. The comrades returned to our camp, and being all three simple fools, they gave implicit confidence to the falsehood contrived to deceive them; and whenever they met their friends and acquaintances they said to them, "Breh! what did we come here for? Our chiefs have sold their country and are now receiving the money for it: we have seen it with our own eyes; why should we stay here? all that passes is but lost labour." By this means they struck with consternation many who were as great asses as themselves, and these spread confusion and alarm through the whole Imperial camp. Finding this pretext of going home, a great number of the troops went off and dispersed, like a flock of young partridges.

The Russian hogs, availing themselves of so favourable an opportunity, brought the devil among us. But the best of the story is, that they all laughed at us in relating it to each other, saying that in order to disperse a Turkish army, they had only to weigh a little gold in the presence of three of their men, and then send them to inform the rest of it. Thus, on account of so many ignorant fools, who understand nothing of the wiles and machinations of the enemy, it is necessary that we should give our troops such a form of discipline as may prevent similar disorders, and the danger of the spies who mix with our men and can never be discovered.

How is it possible for us without such a system, to avenge ourselves of our enemies, to defend our Empire, or to gain the least advantage? As the deep cunning of the Russian race was not at first so well known, our precious heroes of soldiers made use of such expressions. "The Muscovite infidels are dogs of fishermen, whom we can suffocate only by spitting upon them; if we each of us throw a stone, we shall destroy them all." These Janissaries who are merely vain boasters, good only for swaggering on the pavements, falling by thousands into the hands of the Russians through their total ignorance of military affairs, at length saw and learned the power and stratagems of the enemies of our faith. But to what purpose? since the children and daughters of so many noble and pious persons of the Mahometan community have continued even to this day (a space of nearly forty years!) in the possession of the Russians; and the children whom they have produced remain depressed and afflicted, a weeping prey in the hands of soldiers, officers, and other reprobates.[100]

If a rabble of men, ignorant of the world, who pass their whole time in festivity and play, or in buying and selling, or in idleness, were in the first place to learn thoroughly the things which belong to purity, and then, in order to preserve their religion unsullied, were to avoid discourse with infidels and designing men, and examine whether their own observance of it did not require some correction, there is no doubt that they might attain to the summit of the good things, both of this world and of the world to come. If they contend with us, saying, "We understand questions of purity, we preserve our religion, and there is no doubt of the validity of our marriage contract[101]"; in that case, although what they maintain be true, yet, as the knowledge of the affairs of this world is apt to occasion many great sins, let them not lengthen their tongues on a subject of which they certainly know nothing, and to which their understandings cannot reach. If this business of the Nizam-y-Gedid seem obscure to them, let them acquire information from men who, like this humble individual[102], have reached their eighty-seventh year, and have gained by experience a thorough knowledge of the world, and have brought to light what things have injured, and what have turned to the profit of, the Sublime Government. Let them not talk of things void of sense, for as the troubles of man proceed from his words, so reason is given him as a defence against his words.

SECTION VIII.

Many simple persons, who do not know why the treasure of the Nizam-y-Gedid was instituted, and whence this money is collected, and to what purpose it is expended, say sometimes, "the water of the old cistern is not exhausted; why then is the new revenue made a separate treasure?"[103] We have already stated how difficult a thing it is to explain public affairs to people who are plunged in the darkest ignorance, and to make those who cannot read the common alphabet understand science; although we were to labour until the day of judgment, we should not succeed. If a man is capable of receiving the words of truth from his outward ears into his mind, we proceed to relate matters as they really are.

Wars have been carried on for seventy or eighty years in a rude manner, and with weak and irregular troops, during which time the followers of Islam having been often defeated, His Highness Sultan Suleÿman Kannuni thought proper to form the body of the Janissaries, whom he divided into different divisions, assigning to each their particular regiments and quarters. He considered, however, that these troops could not be assembled and kept together for the love of God only, but that it was also necessary to establish funds for the purpose of providing meat, drink, &c. for them, as well as to appoint them a pay suitable to their expenses. After consulting with the wise and experienced men of the time, he regulated the administration of the revenue in the following manner. A small part of the monies drawn from the provinces that had, by right of conquest, become subject to his illustrious predecessors, was appropriated to the subsistence of military men who served on horseback and otherwise. The Emperor appointed by the canon[104] that, from the annual product of the revenues, and from the sums which every one who succeeded to the farming of them, paid according to his means, as an anticipation price, provision should be made for meeting the expense incident to these corps, whether in war or in peace. After these arrangements had been made, it frequently happened that, in good times, no war took place for twenty years together, during which some of the military men who belonged to the corps, having turned old, departed in peace. As the papers granted them to enable them to draw their pay fell into the hands of their servants, relations, or comrades[105], it was not suffered that the allowances appointed for several thousand men should be received by persons who did not belong to the military profession, who were novices in affairs, or apprenticed to some trade. As few of them left sons capable of taking the place of their fathers, and opposing the enemies of our faith, men of war became very scarce, and it was therefore necessary to levy fresh troops, and assign new funds for their support, the old revenue being exhausted. Besides this cause of the impoverishment of the royal treasury, the price of all commodities had greatly augmented since the time that the canon was promulgated. For instance, at that period an oke of the flesh of mutton was sold for four aspers, but in the course of time it rose to twenty-five paras, and other things were dearer in proportion. Thus an increase having taken place in the price of the necessaries which were furnished to the corps at its institution, the royal funds provided for that purpose were no longer able to meet the expense of the times, and as they were nevertheless obliged to find some means of going on, the rents of the Sublime Government began to run into each other; that is to say, that in order to provide for the expense of the current year, they sold the revenue of the succeeding one, and so on. Hence resulted a deficiency in the Imperial finances. Even the treasures, which had been amassed with a great deal of trouble previous to the Russian war that broke out during the reign of the late Sultan Mustapha, were in that war entirely drained and consumed, although every thing was then very cheap when compared with present prices, and after peace, the finances could not recover themselves, but the expense still exceeded the revenue. The enemies of our religion being informed of our want of money, were thereby confirmed in their purpose, and obtained complete success. But besides the difficulties in which our government found itself involved in peaceable times, owing to the deficiency of the ordinary revenue which did not suffice for the current expenses, there have been moments during war in which it stood like a man who has both his hands tied down to his sides, and knew not which way to turn itself; for as there was no ready money, nothing could be accomplished, and nobody showed any inclination to engage in a holy war; nothing was considered but pay, rations, and the privilege of being exempted from active service.

Thus hath the want of a well-organised system of finance been clearly proved, the whole revenue of the state not being sufficient for the exigencies of these times. The following example will point out the truth of this to the people at large. Suppose the case of a man, who twenty or thirty years ago enjoyed an income of one piaster a day, and regulated his expenses accordingly, if that man continued on the same scale how could he live at present, when every thing is four or five times dearer than at that period, and make the two ends of the year meet with his piaster a day? In like manner, we may apply this consideration to the actual condition of the Sublime Government. Behold, while the royal finances are in so great a state of penury, not a single person, whether rich, poor, or tributary subject, will give a single piaster to the treasure, under the name of a voluntary contribution, towards carrying on war; and, in short, no man will go to war gratis, and at his own expense, only to please God, or for the love of the prophet or the emperor; the formation of troops proportioned to those of the enemy, and the providing of military stores, which may equal theirs, are things which must be accomplished, not by words, but by money. The truth is, that the treasury does not possess a fixed revenue sufficient to defray contingent expenses, and, to sum up all, the old revenues of the Sublime Government were calculated for the old expense; and as two hundred and forty-five years have elapsed since the publication of the canon, the expense having constantly increased whilst the revenue was never augmented, His Highness, the Emperor, has looked out for some remedy in such difficult circumstances, and has laboured to establish a revenue proportioned to the amount of expenditure of these times. But that the requisite funds might neither be taken by violence, nor derived from casual contingency, it was thought proper to draw them from the peculiar possessions of the government and the sources dependent thereon. A treasure having been with much difficulty amassed, in which were to be deposited the money raised under the title of Iradi-Gedid, the following reflections presented themselves relative to the manner in which they were to be regulated.

The produce of the imposts at the time that the canon was promulgated, was farmed out in small branches to those who bid for them the highest, and authority was granted to them to receive each a part of the tribute on their advancing a certain sum in proportion to their respective means, and on condition of their paying a thousand piasters a year to the crown besides; thus a man was able in three years to reimburse himself of the small sum which he had advanced, and then if the contract was continued to him for the course of his life, he could make a clear profit of forty or fifty thousand piasters; and perhaps of an hundred thousand if he lived long enough. The contractors continuing to give the crown only a thousand piasters after the first small sum advanced, the whole benefit of the revenue accrued to them, but the profits of the public treasure were not augmented and continued the same. A new method having, therefore, been found absolutely necessary, has been adopted, and in such a manner as to leave no person any pretext for complaint. The arrangement is this: that when the perception of an impost, which belongs by right to the treasury, falls vacant, it is no longer farmed out in consideration of a small sum, but is taken possession of on the part of the Sublime Government, and the management of it is carried on for the benefit of the new treasury; the sum which continues to be paid to the crown, as well as the profits derived from the perception of the impost, are appropriated to the pay, clothing, and allowances of the troops of the Nizam-y-Gedid, and to the special exigencies of the war department, such as the providing of cannon, ammunition, tents, camp equipage, military stores, and the expenses of the park and train of artillery.

As the accountants of the old treasury are wholly employed in the collection and management of the funds appertaining to it, a director was specially appointed for the purpose of watching over that part of the administration, and by his ability the whole has been properly regulated. These are then the advantages which result from the expense of the troops being defrayed by this new financial arrangement. The old revenue hath not been thereby prejudiced, and the charges of the new troops are provided for. This business has been conducted in so masterly a manner that no just cause is left to any one to cry out against it; and the new revenue, like the new system of discipline, being established on the best footing, causes no loss or damage to any man, but, on the contrary, tends manifestly to perpetuate, until the last day, the duration of the empire and of the people of Islam, as must be evident to all persons endowed with penetration.

When we have by so distinct an exposition rendered all these points clear, those men who are acquainted with the difference between alum and sugar, good and bad, and in whose essence is a leaven of science, will, no doubt, listen to reason, and, by Divine grace, being brought under conviction, will submit themselves to the book of God, mighty and powerful!

THE END.

1. A great Roman pavement is still visible in Wallachia. It begins at a small town called *Caracalla*, situated near the borders of the Danube, about three miles from the place where the great river Olt falls into it: and it runs up in a straight line with this river, as far as the Carpathians, where its traces are lost. It probably led to the Dacian capital, Zarmiss, which is now a Transylvanian town, and contains many ruins of Roman monuments of an inferior kind. The Latin language is almost the only one spoken by its present inhabitants.

2. Antonii Bonifici Asculani Rerum Hungaricarum Decades. Decad. ii. lib. 8.

3. Knolles's History of Turkey, p. 204. and Tounousli's, Ισορια Ιης βλαχιας, p. 247.

A piaster and a half is equal to an English shilling.

4. Knolles's History, p. 296.

5. Dracula in the Wallachian language means Devil. The Wallachians were, at that time, as they are at present, used to give this as a surname to any person who rendered himself conspicuous either by courage, cruel actions, or cunning.

6. Although the amount of the tribute was often increased under the successive Voïvodes, the same formalities of payment existed as late as the year 1716, when various changes took place in the Wallachian government, as will be observed hereafter.

7. Nobles.

8. Christian tributary subjects.

9. A Ferman is a written order issued by the Grand Vezier in the Sultan's name.

10. Higher clergy and nobility.

11. Cantimir's History of the Ottoman Empire, p. 186.

12. Cantimir's History of the Ottoman Empire, p. 451.

13. Cantimir's History, p. 452.

14. Chamberlain.

15. "It has been supposed that the Turks, to console the Greek descendants of the imperial family for the loss of empire, had bestowed on them the government of the two principalities of Wallachia and Moldavia, an error which appears to have no other foundation than the assumption of the illustrious name of Cantacuzenus, by two persons of obscure family, born in

Wallachia, who were raised to the administration of that principality in the seventeenth century." Thornton's present State of Turkey, p. 385, from Cantimir's Ottoman Hist. p. 371.

16. A descendant of the Voïvode's grandson above alluded to, is now living in Wallachia, and possesses all the landed property left by his ancestor, which gives him an annual income of upwards of 200,000 piasters. He is looked upon by his countrymen as the first and richest Boyar of Wallachia, and is acknowledged by the court of Vienna as prince of the Roman Empire, a title which, however, he cannot assume in his own country so long as the Turks are the possessors of it.

17. The formulæ of a Beratt will be found in the Appendix, No. 1.; it is the literal translation of the one given to the author by the present Sultan, shortly after his appointment to the official situation in the principalities. The original is written in golden letters, on a very long sheet of parchment, lined with green silk, and containing a variety of curious and rich ornaments.

18. Thornton's present State of Turkey, p. 410.; and Cantimir's Ottoman History, p. 189.

The Russian court was the first who entered into official intercourse with the Greek princes, and styled them by the title of *Hospodars*, from the Slavonic and Russian word *Gospodin*, or Lord. The Greeks, however, having the right to the title of prince from that of Beÿ conferred on them by the Sultan, on their nominations to the principalities, assume that of reigning princes, though they have only the power and prerogatives of Viceroys. They also claim that of *Serene Highness*, which the court of Vienna alone has consented to give them. Their subjects invariably give them that of υχηλοτατε most-high. Their sons are called by the Turkish title of Beÿ-Zaaday, literally meaning prince's son; their grandsons have no title.

19. The Prince Callimacki has sent by me a copy of his code to the university of Oxford. As Dr. Macmichael, in his "Journey from Moscow to Constantinople," gives an account of this book, I abstain from any observations upon it.—*Note of the Author.*

20. In page 416, of the "Present State of Turkey," Mr. Thornton says, "The Boyars of the most ancient families, indeed, assert that they are the descendants of the Slavi, and are of a distinct race from the people who have sprung from the alliances of the Romans with the original Dacians; but the chief distinction among the nobles is their wealth and possessions. The great majority of the Wallachian and Moldavian nobility owe their creation to the Sultan's Voïvodes; for even these ephemeral beings, these fleeting shadows of royalty, are presumed to confer by their breath a permanency of dignity," &c. I perfectly agree with Mr. Thornton as to the latter part of this

observation; but at the same time I must beg leave to say, that although I am well acquainted with all the Boyars who are considered to belong to the most ancient families, I never could discover that their claims to antiquity went beyond the period of Raddo Negro's and Bogdan's establishment; nor indeed are there many sufficiently conversant with the history of their country, or with any other, to know that the Slaves ever came into it, or even that a nation of that name ever existed. Those who call themselves the oldest families merely date their origin from Voïvodes, who have reigned within the last five hundred years; and upon such origin alone they form their claims to ancient nobility.

21. £360,000. sterling.

22. The same who was Captain Pashah at Constantinople in 1810–11, and distinguished himself in that station by so many acts of cruelty.

23. In 1811, mineralogists were sent from St. Petersburgh to explore the Carpathian mines. They discovered some large veins of gold, silver, and quicksilver: time, however, was requisite to put the work into proper train; and when it offered the best prospect of success, peace was concluded, the Russian authorities withdrew, and the mines were filled up again, to remain in their former state.

24. A killow (Constantinople measurement) is equal to an English bushel.

25. One oke is equal to 2⅘ lbs. English.

26. The kintal weighs 44 okes.

27. 40 paras make a piaster.

28. The Fannar is a district of Constantinople, where all the Greeks who enter the career of the principalities reside. They are thus distinguished from the other Greeks of the capital.

29. See Appendix, No. 2.

30. Thornton's Present State of Turkey, p. 434.

31. A declaration of war of the Sultan must receive the sanction of the Mufti, as chief of the religion, who makes his approbation known by a manifesto called *Fetvaa*.

32. He was first interpreter to the embassy; he has since the peace entered the Russian service, and is now attached to the Emperor's embassy at Constantinople in the same capacity.

33. The word "Seraglio" is generally supposed in England to apply exclusively to a palace in which the Grand Signior's women are kept. This idea, however, is erroneous; the Sultan's residence in town is called

"Seraglio." His women, indeed, reside also within its walls, but their apartment is called "Harem." The seraglio occupies the whole extent of ground on which the city of Byzantium stood, and is surrounded by the original Byzantine walls.

34. New military institution, explained in the Appendix, No. 5.

35. Mr. Adair.

36. Sir Arthur Paget had made a fruitless attempt in 1807.

37. Letter addressed by the Emperors Alexander and Napoleon to the King of Great Britain, dated at Erfurth, October, 1808, and official correspondence that followed it between the ministers of foreign affairs of the three sovereigns.—Official Papers published in 1809.

38. The same whose premature appointment in 1805 had partly given rise to the misunderstanding at Constantinople.

39. Corporals.

40. See the Appendix, No. 3.

41. See the Appendix, No. 4.

42. Voltaire's Philosophical Dictionary, vol. iv. p. 199.

43. "It may be questioned whether it ever entered into the contemplation of the Russian cabinet to ameliorate the condition of the inhabitants of Wallachia and Moldavia, since no instance can be produced of any exertion of influence on the part of the Russian consuls to alleviate the distresses of the people, to check and restrain the tyranny of the Greeks, or to promote any plan of permanent benefit to the oppressed inhabitants."—*Thornton's Present State of Turkey*, p. 435.

Mere motives of good-will on the part of the Russian cabinet, are certainly questionable; but several instances of interference have occurred. In the official note given as a declaration of war in 1789, by the Turkish government to the Russian envoy, the composition of which was then attributed to the English ambassador, Sir Robert Ainslie, one of the principal grievances alleged was the conduct of the Russian consul-general at Yassi, who, it was said, had abused the right of interference in a most insulting manner. It may be supposed that the consul had acted in conformity to instructions from his court, who sought to create motives for a rupture; but after the conclusion of pence, nearly the same line of conduct was continued by his successors: I have seen many official documents which prove it; and during my residence in the principalities, several instances have occurred, within my observation, of very active exertion on the part of Russia to keep the accustomed system of extortion in restraint, and to relieve the inhabitants from oppression; and such exertion has certainly on many occasions prevented the condition of the inhabitants from becoming worse.

44. Whenever the Russian or Austrian armies have entered the territory of the principalities in their wars against Turkey, the natives have immediately joined them. At the beginning of the war in 1806, Bukorest was garrisoned by about 10,000 Turks, who declared themselves determined to make a desperate stand against the Russians, and to burn the city, if they should finally see the impossibility of preventing them from taking possession of it. Some inhabitants gave information of this plan to the Russian commander-in-chief Michaelson, who immediately despatched to Bukorest a corps of 6000 men under the command of General Miloradovith, which, by forced marches arrived suddenly before that city, and three days previous to the time they were expected by the Turks. These latter were seized with consternation; all the inhabitants rose against them, and some armed with sticks, others with bricks, tongs, pokers, daggers, swords, and with every thing, in short, that came within their reach, they fell upon the poor Ottomans without mercy, and cleared the town of them as the Russians were entering it. More than 1500 Turks were left dead in the streets, and the Cossacks, who preceded the regular troops, soon reduced them to a state of nudity, in which they remained exposed to the view of the public some hours after tranquillity and order had been restored.

45. The treaty of Yassi signed in 1792, binds the Porte to consult the Russian ambassadors on the choice of the Hospodars, and to appoint none but such as are approved of, or recommended by, the embassy. It contains also the stipulation of their remaining seven years at the head of the principalities.

46. The Prince's daughter.

47. The author alludes to the Sultan and the body of Orthodox Mahometans.

48. The late Sultan Abdullhammid.

49. Died.

50. The Christians.

51. Turkey.

52. 1770.

53. He is called Kannuni from the new canon, or system of military administration which he established, and is the same whom we call 'Solyman the Magnificent.'

54. True believers.

55. Lower order of grocers.

56. The common Janissaries usually follow these trades.

57. There is a tribe of Courdes so called.

58. A kind of soldiers in Asia.

59. Oriental Metaphor.

60. The Christian kings are so called from the Servian word Cral or Prince. More honourable titles are given to Mahometan sovereigns, and to the King of France, who has secured to him by treaty, that of emperor.

61. Christian Europe.

62. America.

63. A form of deprecation, as much as to say, "May the devil take no advantage of the suggestion."

64. 1792, A.D.

65. It would appear that this person had returned from an embassy to Turkey.

66. The author seems here to allude to the Empress Catherine, and to some project that had been laid before her of completing the conquest of Constantinople.

67. Western or European Christians.

68. The Empress.

69. The Archipelago.

70. These reservoirs are situated among the hills and woods between the Black Sea and Propontis, in the forests of Belgrade and Domouzdéré.

71. The author of the project most probably meant the taking possession of the reservoirs, and suspending the course of the waters to Constantinople.

72. It is believed that the Empress Catherine had formed the plan of a similar expedition, and that her death prevented its timely execution. When in 1812, the approaching war between France and Russia rendered the cessation of hostilities, on the Turkish frontiers, absolutely necessary to the future operations of the Russians against the French, it had been determined, and measures were taken accordingly, that an army composed of regular troops, marines, and militiamen, amounting to fifty thousand men, under the command of the Duke of Richelieu, should have been transported from Sevastopol in the Crimea to Domouzdéré, where its landing was to be effected under the protection of a fleet, commanded by Admiral Bailie. This army was to take possession of the reservoirs, and the Turks by whom the event would have been perfectly unexpected and unforeseen, would, no

doubt, have been compelled to sign peace immediately. This bold scheme was to have been executed in case any new difficulties had arisen in the negotiations of Bukorest. It has been kept so secret, that it is doubtful whether any Turk suspects, even at the present day, its having been conceived and seriously intended.

73. A Turkish proverb.

74. The deceased Sultan.

75. Teryak, formerly an article of trade coming from Venice, is supposed in Turkey to be a remedy against the bite of snakes.

76. The titles of some superior officers amongst the Janissaries.

77. A corps of gardeners for the Seraglio, but at the same time the Sultan's body-guards.

78. Regiment.

79. Mahometan priest.

80. The Thracian Bosphorus.

81. These are proverbial expression to denote the vicissitudes of fortune.

82. The Janissaries.

83. Before the institution of the Janissaries, the corps employed in war were chiefly called Segbans.

84. Hagee-Bektash, whose memory is reverenced by the Turks.

85. The Christian Sovereigns of Europe.

86. Markwick Markham, a London watch-maker, in great esteem with the Turks.

87. 7 or 800 leagues.

88. Men of sense.

89. A kind of confection sold in the streets of the principal towns in Turkey, made of paste, butter, and honey.

90. An epithet of disdain, bestowed upon Christians in general.

91. The honour of the Turkish regiments is attached to the preservation of their kettles.

92. The Turks call the head-quarters of a corps, as well as their posts and guards, hearths, as coffee is always made there.

93. In the reign of Sultan Selim, the petty governors of Thrace revolted, and committed great disorders, even menacing the neighbourhood of Constantinople. The city of Adrianople took part with them. The new troops were sent against them, but did not obtain so much success as the author is willing to attribute to them.

94. Men, commonly dervises, who relate stories to amuse people at coffee-houses, and who receive a pecuniary recompense from the auditors.

95. It also means infidel, but it has the sense of reproach or insult.

96. This has happened to them at Zenta, Craoul, Rimnik, Hotim, and Aboukir.

97. Peter the Great. The epithet of mad is in Turkey considered as a compliment to those who distinguish themselves by courage and bravery.

98. Meaning the Author.

99. Domouz, and pezevenk in Turkish, are common epithets which mark disdain.

100. I have seen and conversed with Turkish women in Russia, married to Russian officers who had made them prisoners, and who assured me that they were very highly satisfied with their condition, and felt not the least desire to return to Turkey.

101. The Turks consider the marriage contract to be so intimately connected with religion, that a man who has committed any grievous infraction of their law, is obliged to renew his profession of faith and marriage ceremony, both of which have been rendered void by it.

102. The Author.

103. This is a *jeu de mots*, as Hazinay means in Turkish, both cistern and treasure.

104. The military and financial regulations of the Sultan Suleÿman are contained in a book entitled Kanuni-Humayoun, or Imperial-Mandate.

105. The Janissaries can easily alienate their pay, suffering others to draw it in their name by presenting these documents.